The Other Side of Darkness

Ora Matheny-Jackson

ISBN: 978-0-9766650-4-5

In memory of my Grandmother Odelia Kidd, Mother Sarah Matheny, all my uncles and aunt; Ralph Kidd, L.C. Kidd, Cleavon Kidd, Hershey Kidd, Tommy Kidd, Dempsey Kidd, and my grandson, Khayden Harris.

This world was never my home,

I was just passing through,

Tomorrow I will be leaving,

I will pack a few essentials.

I have been establishing a permanent residency.

Jesus said, "Don't hoard treasure down here where it gets eaten by moths and corroded by rust or worse stolen by burglars.

Stockpile treasure in heaven, where it's safe from moths and rust and burglars.

The place where your treasure is,

is the place you will most want to be and end up being." (Mathew 6:19-21).

"If you don't leave your past in the past,

It will destroy your future.

Live for what today has to offer,

Not for what yesterday has taken away."

"Author Unknown"

Acknowledgements

My heartfelt gratitude to all my dear friends, Sandra Jameson, Debra Rockymore, and Annise Lewis, whose support and attentive ears have been a constant source of comfort and strength in my life.

Thank you for being there to listen when I needed it most, for your patience, empathy, and understanding. Your willingness to lend an ear, often without judgment or reservation has provided me with a safe space to express my thoughts and feelings.

To Marsha Williams, whether in moments of joy or times of sorrow, your presence has been a steadfast anchor, helping me navigate the complexities of life.

To Coleman Hughley, who is like my big brother, you have taught me the true meaning of support and compassion.

I am profoundly grateful for each of you, and I cherish the bond we share. Thank you all for being such an integral part of my journey.

The Other Side of Darkness

Prologue:
The Plan

In the heart of Union Mississippi, 1957, Nya's parents welcomed her into the world. However, fate had plans beyond what anyone could foresee. Her parents, she imagined, dreamed of raising her in the warmth of Union, Mississippi, surrounded by family and the comforting familiarity of southern life. But circumstances intervened. Her Grandma Odessa, who she called Mama, had plans to settle in Chicago, saw the need to take Nya north. She was the beloved child of Stella and Henry. But there was another side to Nya that no one knew about – a side hidden behind the façade of her cheerful demeanor. Deep within her heart, she carried a secret burden, a past filled with shadows and unanswered questions.

As far as Nya could remember, she had never seen her mother and father together. Her earliest memories were of her mother giving her the phone where she would listen to the distant voice on the other end. But there was always a lingering emptiness, a void that she could not understand. It was as if a piece of her life puzzle were missing, and she did not know where she belonged. Nya had always wondered about him, and her curiosity only grew stronger. She would spend hours poring over old photographs, studying the face of the man she barely knew, searching for any clues that might unlock the mystery of his absence.

Nya was a bright and inquisitive child, her mind always buzzing with questions and her heart yearning for answers. Growing up without her father, she often found herself lost in a sea of wondering, who was he? Where was he? And why had he never come around? As she watched other children play with their fathers at the park or share stories about their dads at school, she could not help but feel a pang of longing deep in her chest. She longed for that connection, that bond that eluded her no matter how hard she searched. But try as she might, Henry remained a distant figure, a ghostly presence hovering at the edge of her consciousness. She wondered if he ever thought of her, if he knew the ache that gnawed at her heart with each passing day. By the time Nya turned eight, all she knew of Henry was what she heard and seen in faded photographs her mother had tucked away in an old album.

It was during these solitary moments that Nya's true self emerged, her mask slipping away to reveal the vulnerabilities she kept hidden from the world. In the privacy of her thoughts, she grappled with the echoes of a painful past – a past scarred by loss and longing. There were nights when Nya would stand by the window, gazing out at the star-studded sky, her eyes reflecting the silent tears that traced the paths down her cheeks. She would whisper secrets to the moon, confessions of dreams deferred and promises left unfulfilled.

But amongst the darkness that threatened to engulf her, there flickered a tiny ember of hope – a hope that whispered of new beginnings and second chances. And it was this hope that kept Nya going, propelling her forward with quiet determination. In the end, it was not the mask she wore for the world that defined her, but the courage to embrace the other side of herself – the side that had been waiting patiently in the wings, ready to step into the spotlight and shine. And as Nya stood at the threshold of a new dawn, she knew that the best was yet to come, for she had finally found the freedom to be authentically, unapologetically herself.

Chapter 1:
A Bold Move

Grandma Odessa was married to a man name Robert, a hardworking man with a spirit as restless as the wind. But without warning, Robert left for Chicago early on leaving behind Hank, Troy, Raymond, Lance, Calvin, and Diana, six of their seven children. Stella had married and left home by this time to start her own family. Nya Matthew was the first grandchild of Grandma Odessa. She felt like Nya's mother Stella and father Henry had married too young and did not know the first thing about taking care of a baby. She felt like they were kids themselves. Although Grandma had plans of her own, she could not stop thinking about her only grandchild.

Hank, at sixteen, was now the oldest at home. He had a keen sense of responsibility, stepping into a fatherly role after their father left. Troy, fourteen, was a dreamer of the family. He had an insatiable curiosity about the world beyond Mississippi. Diana at eleven was the heart of the family. She had a nurturing spirit and often helped Grandma with her brothers. Raymond, who was ten, who thought nothing but his appearance and how he looked, energetic and always on the move. His good nature and infectious laughter always won everyone over. Lance, nine, was the quite observer. Though less outgoing than his siblings. Calvin, the youngest at eight, was the smart one who loved to read.

Grandma felt life without Robert was like a shadow cast over her heart. She tended to their home and worked in the fields, all the while yearning for the day when she would reunite with her husband. But as months turned into years, Robert's absence became a heavy burden she carried with her daily.

With determination burning in her soul, Grandma made a decision that would change the course of her life. She resolved to find her husband. She knew that he had relatives that lived in Chicago, so she contacted them. She also knew people who told her to contact them when she arrived. It was a bold move for a woman of her time, but Grandma was driven by love and the unwavering belief that her family belonged together. She decided to make the journey for a chance at a brighter future for her family. Grandma was on a mission to find Robert.

In the sweltering summer of 1957, Grandma

left her home in Philadelphia Mississippi with dreams of a better life for her family. She had grown up in a small, segregated town where opportunities for Black people were limited, and racial tensions ran high. But she carried with her strength and an unshakable belief in the possibility of change. Chicago was her destination, a city of towering skyscrapers and bustling streets, far removed from the cotton fields and dirt roads of Philadelphia Mississippi. Grandma had heard stories about the city, where the winds of progress blew stronger, and the promise of equality seemed more real.

When the train finally pulled into Chicago's bustling Union Station, her eyes widened with wonder. She stepped off the train at Union Station, clutching a worn suitcase filled with her few possessions and a heart full of hope. The city was a whirlwind of activity, with people of all backgrounds and cultures going about their daily lives. Tall buildings reached for the sky, and the streets were alive with the sounds of honking cars and hurried footsteps.

Grandma contacted a lady by the name of Ms. Greene who promised to let her stay with her and her family until she was able to find a place to live. Ms. Greene lived on the West Side in a little house that was set way back from the street. The neighborhood was a mixture of Black and White people. Whites ran stores, except for one store, a Black family owned the store that sat on Kedzie and 15th Street. Joe's Grocery Store was where all the Black folks in the neighborhood would go for groceries. Grandma found that trying to find employment was a challenge, but she was determined to make a new life for her family. One day she saw an advertisement in a local newspaper for a housekeeper position on the South Side. She called to set up a meeting for the job.

Back then Chicago had trolley buses *(electric buses that drew power from a pair of wires strung over the street wire.)* The buses were old and creaky, but they accelerated quickly, they were quiet and did not belch smoke. Grandma took the bus to go to her interview from the west side to the south side of the city. The lack of air conditioning in the summer with the fast speed created lots of breezes through the open window.

When Grandma arrived for the interview, a stern-looking white woman with gray hair greeted her and gave her a thorough once-over before finally nodding in approval. The house was a big house, decorated with pictures of old white folks from the 1800s and tailored drapes hanging on the windows. Mrs. Magaret Carrington needed a tenacious and hardworking housekeeper.

"Hello," said Mrs. Carrington.

"Hello Mrs. Carrington, my name is Odessa King," Grandma responded.

Mrs. Carrington was initially hesitant about hiring Grandma, but there was something in Grandma's eyes that made her take a chance. Grandma's job was to clean, cook, and take care of the household. As the days turned into weeks, Grandma and Mrs. Carrington began to develop an unexpected connection. They would often find themselves talking and sipping tea and sharing stories about their lives.

Mrs. Carrington had lived her entire life on the South Side of Chicago, a city of privilege and comfort, but she had her own struggles. She had been a widow for years and had raised her two children by herself. She had witnessed the racial divide in the city, even in her own neighborhood, and Grandma's stories of life in the South opened Mrs. Carrington's eyes to the harsh realities faced by Black people.

Over time, Mrs. Carrington introduced Grandma to some important people and associates. She invited her to dinner parties, where Grandma would help serve the guests. It was there that she became more than just a housekeeper. Grandma's journey from rural Mississippi to the heart of Chicago was a testament to the strength of the human spirit and the power of unexpected connections.

Mama had come to a new city in search of her husband and a better life for her children and ended up changing the hearts and minds of those she met along the way. Her presence working in that house and her friendship with Mrs. Carrington had a ripple effect on how she was known in the community. Even though she had little education herself, she believed that education and opportunities awaited them in the city, opportunities that she might not find in her hometown. Once she settled in a place, she planned to send for her children.

Chapter 2:
Getting Settled

In 1960 Grandma found a small apartment in a neighborhood on Chicago's West Side on the corner of 16th and Spaulding. The apartment was big enough to house her family nestled among rows of similar houses on a tree-lined street. She settled in the Lawndale neighborhood, where Black families like her were striving for a piece of the American dream. In the sixties, life on the West Side of Chicago was a vibrant area with diversity, resilience, and a sense of community spirit. It was a time of both challenges and triumphs, where neighbors looked out for one another, and the streets busy with the rhythms of everyday life.

The neighbors knew each other by name, and children played freely in the front yards. The sense of community was strong, and Grandma quickly became a part of it. She came to the city for a chance at a brighter future for her family. Each morning, the streets came alive with the hustle and bustle of people making their way to work, children walking to school, and friends greeting each other with warm smiles. On Sundays, churches overflowed with soulful hymns and passionate sermons, serving as pillars of strength and solidarity for the community. Despite the challenges of discrimination and inequality that loomed over the city, the residents of the West Side stood resilient. They formed tight knit bonds, united by their shared experiences and determination to create a better future for themselves and their children.

In the summer, children played stickball in the streets and cooled off in fire hydrant showers, while families gathered in the local parks for picnics and barbecues. On hot days, the ice cream truck made its rounds, its cheerful jingle signaling a sweet relief from the heat. But among the joys of community life, there were also struggles. Economic hardships and racial tensions cast a shadow over the neighborhood, with disparities in housing, education, and employment persisting despite efforts for change. Yet, through it all, the West Side of Chicago remained a place of strength and hope. It was a place where neighbors lent a helping hand, where children dreamed of brighter futures, and where the spirit of community prevailed in the face of adversity.

After settling in the apartment, Grandma's thoughts turned to her children back in Mississippi. She longed for them to join her in the big city. With each passing day, Grandma made plans and preparations, eager to reunite her family under one roof. She imagined the joy of having her children close, their laughter filling the rooms and their presence bringing warmth to her heart. As she made phone calls, Grandma knew that her children's future awaited them in Chicago, but the thought of separation weighed heavily on her mind. In the quiet moments of the evening, Grandma would sit by the window of her apartment, her thoughts drifting back to laughter echoing through the house back in Mississippi. She also wondered how she would cope with the distance, knowing that she would miss watching Nya grow and thrive.

Grandma and Robert had been separated for years, ever since he left coming to Chicago. Her love for him never wavered, and she held onto the hope of reuniting with him one day. She had planned and dreamed about this moment for so long. With determination in her eyes, Grandma set out to find him. She asked around, visited places she had heard he might be. Days turned into weeks, ands still, there was no sign of Robert. Doubt began to creep into Grandma mind, but she refused to give up hope. She continued her search tirelessly, refusing to believe that Robert could be lost to her forever.

However, as time went on, Grandma started to realize that Robert did not want to be found. She imagined he had moved on, started a new life without her. The thought was devastating, but Grandma was a strong woman. She said, "If I can't have my husband, then I don't want no man." Grandma made peace with the possibility of never finding Robert and decided to focus on building a life without him. With her indomitable spirit and determination, Grandma carved out a new path for herself. Though the ache of Robert's absence lingered in her heart, she found comfort in knowing that she was cable of standing on her own two feet. While Grandma never did find Robert, she discovered something even more precious, the power to live her life to the fullest, with or without him by her side. As the day of her children's arrival drew near, she braced herself for the bittersweet reunion though her heart ached with the thought of leaving Nya behind.

A few years later, after everybody had settled in the apartment, Grandma packed her bags and boarded a train bound for Philadelphia, Mississippi. The journey was long, but her excitement fueled her every step of the way. She had decided that she was going to get Nya. She couldn't wait to see Nya and shower her with love and affection.

Finally, the train pulled into the station, and Grandma stepped onto familiar ground. She made her way to Stella's house, her heart fluttering with anticipation. When she laid eyes on Nya, she scooped her into her arms. Grandma stayed for only a few days because she had to get back to work. She had a conversation with Stella and Henry about taking Nya back to Chicago with her and that she had a babysitter available. Stella and Henry did not seem to have a problem with her suggestion. When it was time to go, the day before Stella packed Nya's bags to travel back to

Chicago with her grandma.

Grandma and Nya made it back to Chicago. Stepping off the train onto the platform, Nya was greeted by the bustling energy of the city. The sounds of car horns, distant chatter of footsteps filled the air. Grandma held her hand tightly as they made their way through the busy station. Eventually arriving at Grandma's place that would soon become home was filled with folks talking and laughing. There were family phots adorning the walls and the soft hum of a radio playing in the background. She was content that she had her family together under one roof.

The next day Grandma was on her way to work one chilly morning, her steps cautious as she navigated the icy sidewalks. Despite the bitter cold that seeped into her bones, Grandma was undeterred, her determination unwavering as she braved the elements to provide for her family. As she approached the bus stop, Grandma's breath forming clouds in the crisp winter air, her grip tightened on her worn purse, her thoughts were focused on the day ahead. However, fate had other plans.

With careful steps, Grandma ascended the steps of the bus, her eyes scanning for an empty seat amongst the crowed interior. Just as she reached for the handrail, her foot slipped on a patch of black ice, sending her crashing to the ground with a sharp cry of pain. Time seemed to stand still as concerned voices surrounded her, their words muffled by the ringing in her ears. Through gritted teeth, Grandma fought back tears as she realized the extent of her injury. Her leg throbbed with a fiery intensity, each movement sending waves of agony shooting through her body. Helping hands guided her to a nearby bench, where she sat, her face pale with shock as she clutched her injured limb. The realization slowly dawned upon her that she would not be able to work, at least not for a while until her leg healed.

In the days that followed, Grandma focused all her energy on her recovery, enduring countless hours of pain and discomfort with relentless resolve. Though the road ahead was fraught with challenges, she refused to succumb to despair, drawing from the love and support of her family. As the icy grip of winter began to loosen its hold on the city, so did Grandma determination thaw the obstacles in her path. With each passing day, despite the hardships she faced, her leg grew stronger, her spirit unbroken. With a heavy heart, Grandma knew she had no choice but to seek assistance to support her family during this unexpected setback. As she lay confined to her bed, her leg encased in a cast, worry gnawed at her heart. How would she provide for her family without her steady income? Mrs. Carrington was her solution. With her keen eye for the struggles of others, Mrs. Carrington was quick to offer a lifeline in her time of need.

Mrs. Carrington assured her loyal employee that she did not need to worry about her financial well being. “You’ve worked tirelessly for me and my family for so long,” she said, her voice filled with genuine concern. “Now it’s my turn to take care of you,” and true to her word, Mrs. Carrington continued to pay Grandma her full salary while she recuperated, ensuring that she and her family would not have to endure the hardship of financial strain during this tough time. It was a gesture of generosity that touched Grandma to her core, reaffirming her belief in the inherent goodness of humanity.

As the days turned into weeks and weeks into months, she focused all her energy on her recovery, buoyed by the unwavering support of Mrs. Carrington and her family. And when the time finally came for her to return to work, her leg stronger and her spirit lifted, Grandma did so with a renewed sense of gratitude and purpose.

Eventually, the day came with Grandma was able to return to work, her heart filled with gratitude for the second chance she had been given. Though the scars of that fateful morning lingered, they served as a reminder of her unyielding power of a mother’s love. And as she stepped back onto the bus, her head held high, she knew that no amount of ice could ever extinguish the fire burned within her soul.

From that day forward, the bond between Grandma and Mrs. Carrington grew even stronger, forged not only by the shared experiences of hardship and resilience but also by the enduring power of compassion and generosity. And as she stood side by side in the warm glow of the Carrington kitchen once more, it was clear that their connection transcended the boundaries of employer and employee, it had blossomed into a friendship rooted in mutual respect and care.

Chapter 3: The Apostles

Grandma moved her family to an apartment on Douglas Boulevard across from the park, promised a fresh start filled with new experiences and opportunities. The excitement of moving to a new place mingled with a touch of sadness as we said goodbye to familiar walls and friendly neighbors. But Grandma 's warm smile and reassuring words made it clear that this move was a step forward in the right direction in creating new memories. Douglas Boulevard was a street lined with trees that whispered in the wind and houses that stood like sentinels of history. The new home was a charming, two-story brick house with a wide front porch with two Lions on each side where you could sit and watch the world go by. Across the street, Douglas Park sprawled out in all its green glory, a haven for children and adults alike.

The first day in the new home was filled with activity. Movers carried in furniture and boxes, while we busied ourselves with unpacking and arranging our belongings. The house quickly took on the comforting feel of home, with family photos on the walls and furniture placed in its permanent spot. That evening, after a long day of settling in, Nya and Grandma sat on the front porch, enjoying the cool breeze and the view of Douglas Park. The park was alive with people, children playing, couples walking hand in hand, and groups of friends chatting on the grass. It felt like a world of possibilities right at your doorstep.

In the days that followed, Nya and Grandma explored the neighborhood together. Douglas Park became her playground, a place where she could run, play, and let her imagination soar. Nya spent countless hours there, flying kites with her uncles, and playing catch. As days became months, the park also became a place of community. Nya made new friends with other children from the neighborhood who shared their love of adventure. Together, they explored the park's playgrounds, while some kids played baseball on its field.

One warm Friday evening after Stella got off work, she stopped by and they all gathered on the porch, enjoying the gentle breeze and the chirping of crickets. The porch overlooked the serene Douglas Park, adorned with two majestic stone lions guarding the steps. As dusk settled in, the golden hues of the setting sun cast a warm glow over the scene. Nya sat on top of one of the stone lions, giggling while her uncle Lance told jokes. Stella and Grandma were on the porch just enjoying those special moments. Suddenly, the tranquility was shattered by the sound of rapid echoing through the park. Stella's heart clenched in fear as she instinctively pulled Nya close, shielding her from the chaos unfolding before them. The Apostles gang erupted into violence, running through Douglas Park. The once peaceful park, with its sprawling green lawns and towering trees, became a battleground.

In the chaos, a stray bullet struck one of the stone lions, shattering the peaceful evening. Stella's heart raced with panic as she saw the stone fragment fly, barely missing Nya. For a heart-stopping moment, Stella feared the worst, believing Nya had been struck by one of the bullets. Nya let out a frightened cry clinging to Stella in terror. Her hands were trembling as she quickly assessed Nya, relief flooding her senses when she realized Nya was unharmed.

Tears welled in her eyes as she held Nya close, overwhelmed by the sudden slaughter of danger in the once serene haven. As the gunfire subsided and The Apostles vanished into the night, they remained huddled on the porch, shaken but grateful to be safe and then they ran into the house in case they returned. The wounded lion stood as a stark reminder of the fragility of peace, its damaged eye a testament to the violence that could intrude upon even the most tranquil moments.

By 1964, The Apostles began attempting to organize themselves and stop destroying the community. This movement tapped back into the roots of what The Apostles were originally meant to do and that was to organize the youth to protect the community from undesirable things. In the heart of Chicago's west side, amidst the hustle and bustle of urban life, there existed a community deeply entrenched in the struggles of poverty, violence, and systematic neglect. It was here that The Apostles, once known primarily for their involvement in gang activities, began to undergo a profound transformation.

The Apostles, like other gangs, were born out of necessity. They emerged from the harsh realities on inner-city life, offering a sense of protection and belonging to young men and women who felt marginalized and neglected by society. However, as the years went by, there were some Apostles games members who began to recognize that the cycle of violence and despair plaguing the community needed to be broken. Led by a group of visionary leaders within the gang, The Apostles embarked on a journey to redefine their purpose and impact on the community. They understood that the true strength of their organization lay not in violence, but in their ability to uplift and empower those around them, particularly the youth.

With this newfound mission, The Apostles established programs aimed at providing positive outlets for young people in the neighborhood. They renovated abandoned buildings, transforming them into community centers where children could participate in after school programs, tutoring sessions, and recreational activities. These centers became safe havens where kids could escape the dangers of the streets and find mentorship from reformed gang members who had turned their lives around. But The Apostles did not stop there. Recognizing the need for comprehensive support, they launched initiatives to address the root causes of poverty and crime in their community. They established job training programs, partnered with local businesses to create employment opportunities, and advocated for better access to education and healthcare.

As word of their efforts spread, The Apostles gained support from unlikely allies, including law enforcement agencies and community leaders. Together, they worked to bridge the divide between law enforcement and the community, fostering trust and collaboration in the fight against crime. Despite the obstacles, the West Side community was resilient. Neighbors looked out for one another, sharing food and support in times of need. Church gatherings and block parties provided moments of joy and unity during adversity. The Civil Rights Movement was in full swing, and the West Side played a crucial role. There were protests and marches, fighting for equality and justice.

The Civil Rights Act was signed into law by this time, marking a significant milestone in the fight against segregation. It was a turning point for

Grandma, as she witnessed her own life, and the lives of other Black people begin to change. Slowly but surely, the racial lines that had once divided Chicago were beginning to blur. The Civil Rights Movement had made significant strides, and opportunities were expanding.

Over time, The Apostles' commitment to social change began to bear fruit. Crime rates in our neighborhoods declined, graduation rates rose, and hope restored in a community once plagued by despair. The gang members who once roamed the streets with a sense of aimlessness and anger now walked with a newfound sense of purpose and pride, knowing that they were making a tangible difference in the lives of those of they once called enemies.

The Apostles were heading further in the right direction and established CVL Inc which officially incorporated The Apostles as a legit social services club. They begin to receive government funding to open legit businesses from stores to restaurants to job training a truancy program for the youth. All of this would go south when The Apostles tried to establish more programs that were denied partially because of the investigation into the Greystones gangs mismanaging government funding. The difference with that was The Apostles experience was they were fully willing to use the funds properly and had enthusiasm in the programs.

Chapter 4:
Tough Times

Life on the West Side was not without its challenges. Segregation and racial tension were still prevalent, and poverty was a harsh reality for a lot of families. Grandma, like her neighbors, faced her share of hardships. As some areas in the neighborhood turned from White to Black, the growing population of Black grew quite well as the White's flight was happening in a very rapid succession. One thing that helped "white flight" happen faster was a method called 'blockbusting,' when a real estate agent hires provocateurs to impoverished Black people that wanted to buy homes.

The agent provocateurs would go to the doorsteps of a White family and persuade the family to sell their home at a rock-bottom rate. The agents would tell the homeowners that racial minorities would soon be moving into their neighborhoods. The White folks would be in such a state of panic they would agree to sell fast, not giving themselves enough time to do any research. The agents would then sell those same houses at inflated prices to Black families seeking upward mobility. In the heart of a close-knit neighborhood on Kedzie Boulevard, stood Joe's Store who was a Black owner. It was not just a place to buy groceries; it was the heartbeat of the community. Mr. Joe Allen, a kind and gentle man, had opened the store decades ago and had seen generations of families pass through its doors; among the regular customers was Grandma Odessa. Despite her struggles, she was known for her determination to provide for her family.

Grandma Odessa children were now older and able to contribute to the household. Hank, who was the oldest, and lucky to find a job, spent his days working diligently as a butcher at Joe's grocery store. He stood behind the counter with a quiet confidence that spoke volumes of his expertise. He had a knack for cutting meat and serving customers, earning the respect of the entire neighborhood. His apron stained with the remnants of a hard day's work. Hank greeted each customer with a warm smile and a twinkle in his eye, eager to share his knowledge of all thing's meat related. Despite the long hours and physical demands of his job, Hank approached each day with a sense of pride and dedication that was truly admirable. He took immense pleasure in his work, finding joy in the art of butchery and satisfaction in knowing that he played a vital role in feeding the community he loved.

Next in line was Troy, the enigmatic uncle with a heart of gold, a figure shrouded in mystery yet radiated with love. Though he was not always around physically, his presence lingered in the small gestures and quiet moments that spoke volumes of his affection. He had a quiet demeanor and a stoic presence that seemed to hint at a world of experiences hidden beneath the surface. While Nya's other uncles filled the room with laughter and boisterous tales, Troy observed from the sidelines, his gaze gentle yet piercing, as if searching for something lost in the depths of memory. Despite his absence, Troy made sure to leave traces of his love scattered like breadcrumbs throughout Nya's life. Whether it was the occasional phone call filled with words of encouragement, or a carefully chosen gift that spoke to her deepest desires, Troy reminded her that she was loved and valued beyond measure.

Then there was Lance, Nya's favorite uncle known for his infectious laughter and kind heart. Lance had a way of brightening up even on the gloomiest days, spreading joy wherever he went. He was a man of many talents and passions, and a lover of jazz. With a collection of vinyl records that spanned decades and an encyclopedic knowledge of the genre, he introduced Nya to the mesmerizing world of jazz music at an early age, a time when a kid normally would not be interested. Together they would spend hours listening to the smooth melodies of Nancy Wilson, the soulful rhythms of Miles Davies, and the sultry vocals of Ella Fitzgerald, losing themselves in the timeless allure of the music.

Lance was more than just a connoisseur of jazz –

he was also a pro on the dance floor. With grace and elegance that seemed effortless, he taught Nya as a young girl how to move her feet to the rhythm of the music, introducing her to the art of 'Stepping.' (although back in the day, it was called 'the Bop'). This was a dance popular in Chicago. From the intricate footwork to the subtle shifts in rhythm, Lance patiently guided her through each step, instilling in her a love for dance that would last a lifetime.

Despite his passion for music and dance, Lance was a man who seemed to drift from job to job, never staying in one place for long. His restless and free-spirited nature led him down a path of unpredictability, where the only constant was change itself. But no matter where life took him, Lance was always available for Nya, sharing his wisdom and love for the arts with her every step of the way.

Raymond was the person Nya would run to and tell if anybody was bullying her outside or at school. He was smooth as silk and sharp as a blade. With his chiseled features, impeccable fashion sense, and a smile that could charm the stars from the sky. Raymond was a man who commanded attention wherever he went. But beneath the polished façade lurked a secret world, a world where the stakes were high and the risks even higher. Raymond was a hustler who navigated the shadowy underbelly of the city with the skills of a seasoned veteran. He moved through the smoky backrooms of underground pool halls and seedy speakeasies with the confidence of a man who knew he held all the cards. With a quick wit and a silver tongue, he could talk his way out of any situation, turning the odds in his favor with a flick of his wrist and a winning smile.

But life in the big city was never easy, especially for a man walking the thin line between fortune and ruin. For every big win, there were countless losses lurking in the shadows, waiting to drag Raymond down into despair. Yet, he refused to be deterred, his determination burning bright like a flame in the darkness. With each roll of the dice and every turn of the card, Raymond danced on the edge of danger, risking it all in pursuit of the elusive jackpot that would set him free.

For him, the thrill of the game was not just about the money – it was about the rush, the adrenaline that surged through his veins with each heartbeat. In the quiet moments of reflection, when the lights faded into darkness and the city slept soundly beneath a blanket of stars, Raymond found himself questioning the path he had chosen. Was the allure of the game worth the sacrifices he had made, or had he traded his soul for a fleeting taste of victory?

Calvin, the youngest of the brothers, had a spirit as wild as the wind and curiosity that knew no bounds. He had aways been a restless soul, finding it hard to sit still in the confines of a classroom. Despite the best efforts of his teachers and family, his heart was never truly in his studies. As he embarked on his sophomore year of high school, he found himself increasingly disillusioned with the rigidity of school life. He longed for adventure and excitement, feeling trapped by the monotony of textbooks and lectures. While his classmates diligently attended classes and dreamed of bright futures, Calvin felt suffocated by the weight of expectations placed upon him.

Calvin made a decision that would alter the course of his life. He had decided to drop out of school. His decision sent shockwaves to Grandma, but his mind was made up. Leaving behind the familiar halls of academia, he ventured out into the world with a sense of exhilaration and trepidation coursing through his veins. For the first time in his life, he was free from the constraints of the classroom, free to explore the world on his own terms. But despite the newfound independence, Calvin could not shake the nagging feeling of uncertainty that gnawed at his conscience. As days turned into weeks and weeks into months, he found himself grappling with the consequences of his impulsive decision. There were moments of quiet reflection. Calvin could not help but wonder if he had made a mistake. Had he thrown away his future for the fleeting thrill of rebellion and would he ever find his place in a world that seemed so vast and unforgiving?

Then there was Diana, who took on the role of both Nya's sister and aunt. Diana's path diverged from the traditional trajectory of education early on in her life. Despite her natural intelligence and eagerness to learn, Diana decided to cut her education short by dropping out of school after completing the eighth grade. Armed with a fierce sense of independence and an unwavering work ethic, Diana set out to carve her own path in the world. She took on odd jobs around the neighborhood, from babysitting to cleaning houses, earning a modest income that helped support the family. Though Diana's formal education may have ended prematurely, she never stopped learning and growing as a person.

Grandma was a pillar of the community, known for her warmth and wisdom. Everybody knew and respected her. The children and the gang members would never say anything disrespectful in her presence. She was a force to be reckoned with, with a heart as warm as her kitchen and a work ethic that could move mountains. She had weathered many storms, and her strength had only grown with time. Although, times were tough, and it was often a challenge to make ends meet. Every week, Grandma would visit Joe's Store to buy groceries. She would carefully select items from the shelves and place them in her cart, all the while keeping a watchful eye on her budget. But there were weeks when the expenses became overwhelming, and Grandma would come up a few dollars short. In those moments of despair, she would approach Mr. Joe, who knew her well. With a warm smile, he would ask,

"Ms. King, is everything okay?"

"I'm a little short this week," she responded.

Grandma would recount her struggles with honesty, never asking for charity but hoping for understanding. Mr. Joe, understanding the importance of community, would nod empathetically. He would tell her,

"Don't worry, Ms. King. We'll take care of it."

Joe's Store operated on a system of trust and understanding over the years. While the neighborhood had its share of financial difficulties, Mr. Joe had always believed in helping his neighbors rather than turning them away. In the spirit of kindness and compassion, he would add those few dollars to Grandma's bill, allowing her to provide for her family that week. She would express her heartfelt gratitude and promise to repay Mr. Joe as soon as she could. And she always did, bit by bit. It was not just a transaction; it was a display of community support and a lifeline for Grandma and her family.

As the years passed, Joe's Store continued to be a place of connection and camaraderie for the neighborhood. The people who shopped there were not just customers; they were friends, and Mr. Joe was not just a store owner but a pillar of the community. One day, Mr. Joe decided to retire after running the store for decades. The news saddened the neighborhood, but it was time for him to take a well deserved rest. Grandma came to the store one last time. Tears welled up in her eyes as she looked at Mr. Joe, who had always been there when her family needed him the most.

With a hug and a heartfelt "thank you," Grandma handed Mr. Joe the final payment for the last groceries she had received on credit. It was a symbol of the enduring strength of their bond and the collective spirit of the community. Joe's Store had changed hands, and the legacy of compassion and mutual support had also changed. The new owners could not continue the tradition.

Chapter 5:
Stella

One evening, as the cicadas sang their evening chorus, Nya's mother Stella sat on the porch with Henry, her father. The air was thick with the sweet scent of magnolia blossoms, and the stars twinkled above like distant beacons. Stella decided to follow in her mother's footsteps and set her sights on Chicago.

Stella finally broke her silence, Stella turned to Henry, her eyes filled with a mixture of hope and determination.

"Henry," she began, her voice soft yet resolute,

"I've been thinking a lot about Chicago. It's time for a change, for us."

Henry turned to her, "What do you mean?"

"I mean Chicago," she replied, her eyes gleaming with determination.

"I want a chance at something more. There are opportunities there we can't find here."

Henry's brow creased; uncertainty etched in his expression.

For weeks they debated, weighing the pros and cons. Eventually, they reached a decision. Stella began to plan the move. Stella would venture to Chicago, while Henry would tie up loose ends in Mississippi before joining her. The day of departure arrived, marked by goodbyes, and promises.

When she arrived, the city was quite different from the quiet streets of their hometown. She made it to her mother's house and the reunion was filled with tears, laughter, and warm embraces. Grandma welcomed her with open arms, her face glowing with joy. Everybody was excited to see Stella, including Nya, although she hadn't seen her mother in a while. "Nya!" her voice filled with joy as she scooped up her into a tight embrace. She smiled gently, brushing Nya's hair from her forehead. Stella settled into new surroundings, embracing the vibrant energy of the city.

After months or so had passed, Stella was lucky enough to find work in a factory on the North Side, forged new friendships with kindred spirits from all levels of society and discovered a sense of belonging in the bustling city that had once seemed so daunting. Stella set out to find a place to call her own in the city's west side. Each neighborhood had its own unique charm and character. With a list of potential apartments in hand, Stella began her research in earnest. She explores neighborhoods rich with history and culture from the lively streets of Lawndale. Each apartment she visited held its own allure, but none quite felt like the perfect fit. Stella pressed on, as she continued her quest for the ideal place to lay down roots. And then, one fateful day, she stumbled upon a hidden gem nestled in the heart of Bronzeville off 47th Street, a cozy apartment with ivy-clad walls and a welcoming front porch that beckoned her home. The crowds reflected the people living in the Black Belt, young and old, poor, and prosperous, professionals and laborers.

Stella knew that she had found the place she had been searching for. It was not just an apartment, it was a home, a haven where she could write the next chapter of her life surrounded by the vibrant energy of Chicago. She signed the lease and made Bronzeville her new home. As she settled into her cozy apartment, she felt a sense of peace wash over her, knowing that she had found her place to build a life filled with hope, adventure, and endless possibility. Weeks turned into months, and yet Henry never showed up in Chicago. Stella waited anxiously, hoping for his arrival, but as time passed, she could not ignore the sinking feeling in her gut. She tried to reach out to him, but her calls went unanswered, her letters left unread. With each passing day, the silence between them grew louder, echoing the unanswered questions that lingered in her mind.

As she settled into her new life in Chicago, Stella

could not shake the nagging uncertainty of Henry's absence. She remains tethered to the unanswered mystery of why he never followed through on their plans. Was it fear? Doubt? Or something she could not even fathom? She turned her focus to her new home and a life without Henry. Bronzeville was well known for nightclubs and dance halls. There was jazz, blues and gospel music that developed during the migration of Southern musicians. There was the Regal Theater that hosted the most talented and glamorous Black entertainers. The community was also home to quite of few prominent African American artists and intellectuals like Louis Armstrong and Katherine Dunham.

When Nya was a young girl, she always admired her mother with a mixture of awe and longing. Stella had a presence about her – graceful, stylish, and confident. Whenever Stella visited Grandma's house, Nya would impatiently wait for Stella arrival she would be outside playing, her heart pounding with anticipation as she watched for her familiar figure to appear walking down the street. Nya would spot Stella, her head held high, a soft smile playing on her lips. When Stella finally arrived, she would rush into her arms. Stella's outfits were always impeccable – dresses that flattered her figure, paired with elegant heels that clicked with every step she took. Stella was rarely seen without her towering heels, each step a graceful glide that displayed her beautiful legs. Her hair was always perfectly styled, and she had a way of carrying herself that made Nya think of the women she saw in movies, poses and glamorous. Stella was a vision of elegance and sophistication. With an innate sense of style and a flair for fashion, she effortlessly captured the essence of the era in her wardrobe choices.

Stella's perfume would linger in the air, a scent that Nya would come to associate with comfort and warmth. Stella would bend down to kiss Nya on the forehead, her touch light and affectionate. Nya loved those moments when her mother would sit down with her and Grandma, sharing stories and laughter, making grandma's house feel like the most special place in the world.

She would always bring something for Nya whether it was a can of chocolate pecan candy Katydids to the little wrapped pound cakes. Sometimes Nya would go home with her for the weekend. They would ride the bus to the South Side where Stella lived in a one-bedroom apartment. Although their time was often brief, the memories they created on those shopping trips would last a lifetime, a testament to the enduring bond between a mother and a daughter.

On Saturdays, they would go shopping either on Madison Street or Maxwell Street. They shopped at stores like Three Sisters, Goldblatt, Woolworths and a bunch of other stores on Madison Street. They would set off on their shopping excursions, weaving through the crowded streets as they browsed the vibrant storefronts. They would go into shops filled with colorful dresses, sparkling jewelry, and toys that seemed to stretch to the sky. Maxwell Street, where Peddlers sold goods from the sidewalk stands and pushcarts offering items from clothes to produce to appliances. Shoppers could find anything and everything their hearts desired. They would walk from store to store buying outfits for Nya to wear. Then they would stop at one of the stands and order a "Maxwell Street polish."

As Nya grew older, she found herself wanting to be just like her mother. She admired how Stella always seemed to know what to say, how she could walk into a room and command attention without even trying. Stella's elegance and strength were qualities Nya aspired to, even if she didn't fully understand them at the time.

There were times when Nya would sneak into her mother's room when she visited her, carefully pulling out one of her dresses from the closet. She would twirl in front of the mirror, imagining herself grown up, with the same confidence and style that Stella had. It was in those quiet moments that Nya felt a deep connection to her mother, a sense of wanting to follow in her footsteps.

Stella's visits were always too short for Nya's liking, but they left a lasting impression. She would watch her mother walk back down the street, her heart filled with admiration and a determination to be like

Stella when she grew up. Nya dreamed of the day she would dress like her mother, walk with the same grace, and carry the same strength that Stella did.

Chapter 6:
Bad News

Grandma decided it was time to move again, this time to a bigger four-bedroom apartment on 15th Street. It was a beautiful Greystone building with apartments in the front and rear with families who lived there. The landlord named was Ms. Sallie Mae. She lived on the first floor with her two sons and two daughters. Grandma rented the apartment on the third floor. Ms. Sallie Mae two daughters were around the same age as Nya. The neighborhood had been a crucible of history during that time, a place where ordinary people like Grandma stood up for their rights and created a tight-knit community that supported one another through thick and thin. It was a time when hope and resilience thrived, and the echoes of that era still resonated in the hearts of those who had lived through it, carrying the legacy forward into the future.

Grandma was the matriarch of the family, holding everything together with her unwavering strength and love. Her boys had grown up in the neighborhood where opportunities were scarce. They had seen their mother work tirelessly to provide for them, making sacrifices to ensure they had everything they needed. Despite Grandma efforts and her good intentions, her boys found it difficult to secure stable employment. The economic landscape was harsh, especially for young Black men back then with little education and job opportunities were exceedingly rare. Each rejection and closed door chipped away at their confidence, making it harder for them to keep trying.

Grandma would often shake her head and wonder aloud what had happened to her boys, why they did not share her drive and determination. She somehow kept the family together all by herself. Her children, though, seemed content to lead their lives free from the constraints of the conventional workplace. Each had a unique soul, but the boys inherited a stubborn streak that made them resistant to the idea of finding a job. Though, she never faltered in her efforts to provide for her family, working tirelessly as a professional cook day in and day out, and even attending classes at night at the local high school to improve herself.

Every morning, as the sun began to rise over the neighborhood, grandma would lace up her sturdy shoes and prepare for another day at Sacred Heart Home. The senior citizen facility was just a block away from her house, a short walk that she made every day without fail. Rain or shine, cold or heat, she never missed a day of work. It was a part of her routine, her commitment, and her pride. As the head cook at Sacred Heart Home, grandma was responsible for more than just feeding the residents – she nourished them, both body and soul. She believed that food was more than just sustenance; it was a way to show love, care, and respect. Every meal she prepared was crafted with the same attention to detail and the same passion she would put into a meal for her own family.

She would arrive at Sacred Heart just as the kitchen was starting to come to life. The smell of freshly brewed coffee would greet her as she walked in, and she would immediately get to work. She knew the preferences of each resident – the ones who liked their eggs scrambled just right, the ones who needed their toast lightly buttered, and the ones who had a sweet tooth and would light up at the sight of her homemade desserts. Her colleagues admired her dedication and often remarked on how she never seemed too tired. But for grandma, this was more than just a job. It was her calling.

She understood that the residents at Sacred Heart Home had lived their full lives, that they had their own stories, their own struggles, and that now, in their twilight years, they deserved to be treated with dignity and warmth. And in her eyes, there was no better way to do that than through a hot, delicious meal. As she moved through the kitchen, stirring pots and chopping vegetables, she'd hum softly to herself, sometimes singing an old hymn or a favorite tune from her listening to the radio. Her presence brought a sense of calm to the kitchen, a steady hand in the midst of the hustle and bustle of meal prep. Her coworkers knew that they could count on her, that the meals would always be ready on time, and that they would always be good.

The residents loved her too. They looked forward to her meals, not just because they were tasty, but because they could feel the care that went into them. She knew them all be name, and she made it a point to chat with them whenever she had a moment. She'd ask about their day, listen to their stories, and sometimes, share a bit about her own life. In those moments, the dining hall would feel less like an institution and more like a home. When her shift ended, she would clean up her station, wipe down the counters, and make sure everything was ready for the next day. Then, she'd say her goodbyes and start her walk back home, the same way she had come. The walk gave her a chance to reflect on the day, to think about what she could do better, and to take pride in the work she had done.

Nya, being the youngest in the family, with five protective uncles and one aunt who most people thought were Nya's siblings, was only a few years older than her. She was enveloped in a cocoon of affection by her uncles and aunt. Her five boisterous uncles, each with their own unique personalities, and her aunt, treated her like their own little princess. With their rough and tumbling ways and playful teasing, they made sure Nya felt cherished and protected at every turn. Around the house, Nya's uncles would scoop her up in their arms, showering her with love, while her aunt would fuss over her with gentle care, brushing her long hair and dressing her in frilly dresses to go out to play. To Nya, they were her heroes, her confidants, and her protectors. Her uncles, especially Lance, were ever vigilant and fiercely protective, hovered over her like a guardian angel, wary of any potential harm that might befall their precious little niece. Nya knew that the love and attention showered upon her by her Grandma Odessa and uncles, and aunt was priceless. Nya rejoiced in the warmth and security of their embrace.

Nya was about to turn five years old. Her birthday was approaching, and Grandma wanted to make it a special day for her despite the challenges of time. On the morning of her birthday, Nya woke up to the delicious smell of Grandma's cooking. The kitchen was filled with the aroma of something sweet. As Nya entered the kitchen, her eyes were widening in delight as the sight of a small, homemade cake on the table, adorned with five brightly colored candles.

"Happy birthday!" Grandma shouted, pulling her into a warm hug. "Today is your special day, and we're going to celebrate it in style."

Nya smiled with her heart swelling with joy. "Thank you, Grandma! Can I blow out the candles now?"

"Not yet,' she chuckled. "First, you have to make a wish."

Nya didn't know what to wish for because as far as she knew, she had everything she needed.

Nya often drew attention wherever she went. Whether she was playing outside or heading to school, people couldn't help but notice the way she was dressed and the care that had been put into her appearance. Her clothes were always neat and stylish, often the envy of other children in the neighborhood. She had ribbons in her long hair, polished shoes, and outfits that seemed almost too nice for everyday wear. People would see Nya and think she was such a spoiled brat. After all, who else got to wear such nice clothes just to go outside to play? Who else had uncles and an aunt who showered her with attention and gifts? Some of the other children would tease her, calling her "princess" in a mocking tone, or refusing to play with her because they thought she was too fancy for their games. Nya, for her part, didn't understand why some of the kids were mean to her. She didn't see herself as spoiled – she just felt loved.

When Grandma Odessa registered Nya for school, she started at Howland Elementary school on the West Side. She began kindergarten in the fall of 1962. Nya and her grandma made their way to the school, a red brick building that echoed with sounds of children's laughter and the shuffle of tiny feet. They entered the school's Main Office, where they were greeted by the friendly receptionist, Mrs. Reed, who wore a perpetual smile, and a pair of glasses perched delicately on the bridge of her nose. With kind words and a gentle demeanor, Mrs. Reed helped Grandma Odessa complete the necessary paperwork to enroll me in kindergarten. As they waited, Nya eyes widened with anticipation, taking in the sights and sounds of the bustling school. She gazed at the colorful posters adorning the walls, depicting numbers, letters, and cheerful animals. The air was filled with scent of chalk dust and fresh paper, igniting her imagination with endless possibilities. Soon enough, they were ushered into the kindergarten classroom, where they were greeted by the imposing figure of Ms. Pitts. Towering over her young children, Ms. Pitts was a formidable presence, her long skirt swishing with every step, and her funny-looking shoes tapping against the wooden floor.

Mrs. Nesbitt, the stern yet well-intentioned vice principal of Howland elementary school lived in the same neighborhood right around the corner from Nya on Albany Street. Teachers would often comment on how well put together she was, and some even assumed she came from a wealthy family. But the truth was, Nya's family wasn't rich. They were just incredibly generous with what they had, always making sure that Nya never went without. However, prying or overly protectiveness found its way whenever Nya decided to engage with certain kids on the school playground. Ms. Nesbitt, ever watchful eyes, would catch on with these interactions and promptly place a call to Nya's grandmother, expressing her concerns about the company she was keeping. Nya learned early on that it takes all kinds to live in this world and being friendly to people did not matter how they looked.

Despite her best efforts, Grandma could not help but feel a mix of frustration at the repeated calls from Ms. Nesbitt. Mama knew Nya meant no harm and simply had a knack for befriending everyone, regardless of how other kids looked. Determined to find a solution, Grandma decided to pay a visit to Ms. Nesbitt one afternoon. She sat down with the vice principal to have a heart-to-heart conversation.

"Ms. Nesbitt," she began, her voice gentle yet firm.

"I understand your concerns, but Nya has a big heart. She sees the good in everyone and simply want to be friends regardless of what others might say or think."

Ms. Nesbitt listened attentively, her stern expression softening. Slowly, she began to see me in a different light, not just as a naive child, but as someone with a genuine desire to connect with others. After their conversation, Ms. Nesbitt made a promise to continue to keep a closer eye on Nya, not to scold or reprimand, but to ensure her safety and wellbeing while in school. From that day forward, Nya continued to be the friendly neighborhood kid, playing with whoever crossed her path on the school playground.

Double Dutch was always going on before and after school and every chance she got, you would always find her jumping rope. And whenever Ms. Nesbitt saw her playing or engaged in conversation with someone she might have previously disapproved of, she simply smiled, knowing that Nya's grandmother was just a phone call away.

In 1962, when the Vaccination Assistance Act was passed. It was to achieve as quickly as possible the protection of the population, especially for all school children through intensive immunization activity over a limited period. Grandma Odessa went ahead and registered Nya to have the vaccine. Each day Nya would walk to school by herself, crossing busy Kedzie Street to get to school. Once she arrived, she was greeted by Ms. Pitts standing at the door. Around ten o'clock when the students were all in their seats, she would pass out cookies and milk. Nya would always ask for the four-pack Oreo cookies and a carton of chocolate milk.

The bell rang out, signaling the start of a new day. Nya never misses a day out of school, she was excited about going to school. Rows of eager students filed into the assembly hall, youthful chatter filling the air with energy and anticipation. But today was different. Today, there was a palpable sense of apprehension among the children as we took our seats on the polished wooden benches. At the front of the hall stood nurse Jenkins, a kindhearted woman with a no-nonsense demeanor, carrying a try laden with vials of vaccine. Nurse Jenkin addressed the assembled students, explaining the importance of vaccination in protecting against the dreaded diseases of measles, mumps, and rubella. She spoke of the dangers posed by these illnesses, and the vital role that each child played in safeguarding our own health and the health of our classmates.

As she spoke, a hush fell over the assembly hall, punctuated only by the occasional sniffle or nervous shuffle of the feet. The gravity of the situation weighed heavily on the young minds gathered before her, our wide eyes reflecting a mixture of fear and uncertainty. With a warm smile and steady hands, she began administering the vaccines, one by one, to the brave children who stepped forward. Some children winced at the sting of the needle, while others remained stoic. Nya's grandma was still by her side as well as other parents during this time.

Throughout that year, Nya thrived under Ms. Pitts' guidance. Despite her stern exterior, she possessed a heart of gold and a knack for nurturing young minds. With her patient encouragement and gentle discipline, Nya blossomed into a confident and eager learner, soaking up knowledge like a sponge. From learning the alphabet to making friends on the playground, kindergarten was a magical journey filled with laughter, discovery, and endless wonder.

By the time Nya really got the hang of going to

the school and meeting new kids, Ms. Pitts came in the classroom and announce,

"Everyone have a seat; I have some bad news."

It was November 22, 1963. We all sat in our seats quietly.

"President Kennedy has been shot."

The children were young and did not understand what was going on, so the school dismissed the class and everyone in the school was sent home.

Nya remembered the panic in her grandma's face and what was being shown on the TV. As they both sat down to watch the harrowing events unfold giving insight into the confusion and panicking of the nation as to the news of the fate of the President. The report began with, "PRESIDENT KENNEDY WAS SHOT TODAY JUST AS HIS MOTORCADE LEFT DOWNTOWN DALLAS." It was later confirmed that he died of a gunshot wound in the brain at approximately 1pm.

Chapter 7: An Unbreakable Bond

Grandma Odessa, the woman who raised Nya was her hero, her confidante, and her best friend. Their bond was unbreakable, forged through countless shared experiences and a deep, abiding love. Nya always had childhood flashbacks of many train trips she took with her grandma to visit her father. One of the most cherished traditions Nya had was their biannual trips to Mississippi to visit her grandma's father, whom they called Papa.

Born around 1890, he was a living testament to strength and independence, even as he reached the ripe age of seventy something in the 1960s. Papa lived alone in an old wooden house weathered by years of sun and wind and stood among a sea of towering trees that even stood as a testament to a bygone era. Its rustic charm reflected Papa's rugged spirit. The house, with its weathered boards and creaky floors, was filled with memories and stories that spanned generations. Despite his age, Papa remained remarkably active, still working, and walking to places he wanted to go with a determination that belied his years. His weathered hands bore the scars of a lifetime of arduous work, yet they possessed a strength and resilience that spoke volumes about his character.

Their visits were filled with laughter and love as Papa shared meals, he cooked over an old, wooded stove and spent lazy afternoons rocking on the porch, watching the world go by. In the quiet moments between conversations, as the sun dipped below the horizon and the crickets began their nighty serenade, Nya could not help but feel grateful for the time spent with Papa and listening to his stories. Every visit was a journey into the past, as Papa regaled Nya and Grandma with tales of his youth and the land, he once called his own. As they sat on the porch, the creaking of the wooden floorboards beneath them added a rhythm to Papa's narratives, painting vivid pictures of a different time.

With a twinkle in his eye and a voice tinged with nostalgia, Papa spoke of the sprawling acres he had tended to with sweat and determination. He described the fertile soil that yielded bountiful crops and the towering oak trees that whispered secrets in the wind. But the beauty of his land lurked a shadow of injustice. In hushed tones, Papa recounted how the land he loved dearly was taken from him by those who wielded power and privilege. Papa spoke of the injustices he faced at the hands of the white folk who saw fit to claim what was not rightfully theirs. They exploited his lack of education and manipulated the system to their advantage, leaving Papa with nothing but memories and a deep sense of betrayal. Yet, despite the bitterness that tinged his tales, Papa remains steadfast in his belief that knowledge was the key to empowerment. He urged Nya to cherish her education, for it was a weapon against the injustices of the world.

On a hot July morning at the train station in Philadelphia, Mississippi, Nya, and grandma stood on the platform, waiting for the train that would carry them back home to Chicago. Nya's My heart raced with excitement and a hint of trepidation as the locomotive's whistle echoed through the station. Once on board, they settled into their seats, watching the Mississippi landscape pass by through the train's windows. The rhythmic clacking of the wheels on the tracks lulled her into a sense of calm. Nya felt safe and reassured by the presence of her grandma, who had a lifetime of wisdom and stories to share.

The train ride continued far beyond that day. As a little girl Nya carried the lessons and values instilled in her by her grandma and her southern roots. She often told her in her own southern language that there was a whole wide world waiting to be explored. As the train continued northward, Grandma entertained me with stories, growing up in a time when life was different and more challenging. She spoke of the Great Migration, when countless Black families like theirs had left the South in search of better opportunities and freedom from segregation and discrimination.

Soon, the trips to Mississippi became more poignant. Papa was getting older, and each visit felt more precious than the last. Nya cherished the moments spent in the old wooden house, the stories shared, and the love that bound them together. When Papa passed away, Nya and Grandma mourned deeply, but also celebrated his remarkable life and the legacy he left behind.

Life was vibrant and full of activity. Nya and Grandma did everything together. She tried to teach her how to cook, but Nya was never interested. So, sometimes she just watched. When Grandma started cooking, the kitchen filled with the delicious aroma of cornbread, collard greens, and friend chicken. Her Grandma was her rock, her guiding star. She taught her the importance of family, hard work, and resilience. Her wisdom and love were the foundation upon which Nya built her life. She encouraged her dreams, celebrated her successes, and comforted her in times of sorrow.

Grandma became a symbol of resilience, determination, and the enduring hope for a better future that inspired countless others who, like her, had left their homes in search of new horizons. Every week, without fail, they would gather around the television set, eagerly awaiting the latest episodes of their favorite shows like "My Three Sons," "The Donna

Reed Show," "Petticoat Junction," and "The Beverly Hillbillies" and so many other shows. Their ritual was simple yet precious. Mama pulled out two ice- cold bottles of her favorite Nehi Orange Pops from the fridge. Then she reached into the cabinet and grabbed a handful of salty peanuts dropping them into the neck of each bottle. Nya watched in fascination as the peanuts sank into the bubbly orange liquid, creating a curious concoction that intrigued her taste buds. Grandma chuckled at her expression and handed her a bottle, saying, "trust me dear, you're in for a treat."

As they sipped on their peculiar drinks, Nya curled up next to her grandma on the floral-patterned couch, with anticipation palpable as the opening theme music filled the room. The glow of the TV cast a warm light upon their faces as they immersed themselves in the lives of 'the Douglas' family and 'the Clampetts.' As they watched the antics of Steve Douglas raising his three rambunctious sons or chuckled at the misadventures of the eccentric Clampett clan navigating their newfound wealth in Beverly Hills, Nya and her grandma shared more than just laughter. With each episode, they bonded over shared jokes, heartfelt moments, and the timeless wisdom imparted by the characters.

During commercial breaks, they would discuss the plot twists and speculate on what might happen next, our imaginations fueled by the captivating storytelling unfolding before them. Sometimes, Grandma would share anecdotes from her own youth, reminiscing about simpler times and the parallels she saw between her lives and those portrayed on the screen. Nya grandma's favorite show was the 'Tom Jones' show that came on every Friday night with his booming voice and legendary charisma graced the television screen. Grandma's love for Tom Jones was no secret. She would excitedly clear her schedule, insisting that nothing could interfere with her weekly date with the Welsh heartthrob. Nya could not help but notice the sparkle in Grandma's eyes whenever Tom's songs filled the room, and the way she leaned a little closer to the screen whenever he appeared in those infamous tight pants.

Even as young as Nya was, she found it amusing, this infatuation her grandma seemed to have with the suave singer. Nya often teased her gently, suggesting that Tom Jones had cast a spell on her. Grandma would just laugh and play along, but Nya could tell there was a twinkle of truth in her eyes. Through the laughter and occasional tears, Nya and her grandma forged a deep connection that transcended the confines of their living room. They found comfort and joy in each other's company, their weekly television ritual becoming a cherished tradition that strengthened their bond. Those memories of their special moments spent together will remain etched in Nya's heart forever. Even though the TV shows they loved will become nostalgic relics of a bygone era, the enduring legacy of their shared laughter and love will endure a testament to the enduring power of family and the simple joys of togetherness.

Chapter 8:
Love and Wisdom

As an only child and the sole grandchild, Nya closes companion was her grandma whose love and wisdom shaped her world in a profound way. The days filled with simple joys and cherished routines. Whenever grandma set to work in the kitchen, preparing Sunday dinners or baking delicious cakes and teacakes, Nya would patiently hang nearby, her eyes alight with anticipation, Nya knew that as soon as grandma finished mixing the batter, she would be allowed to indulge in the sweet reward of licking the bowl clean.

It was a small but precious ritual, one that symbolized the warmth and love that permeated their relationship. With each swipe of her finger through the sugary mixture, Nya felt a sense of connection to her grandma, a silent understanding that transcends words. Grandma would cook fried chicken, beans, greens, macaroni and cheese, and meatloaf, but Nya would not eat any of it except for the chicken and macaroni. She didn't care for vegetables at all. As they waited for the cakes to bake or the savory aromas of Sunday dinner to waft through the house, Grandma would tell stories of her own childhood in the South. With a twinkle in Nya's eye and a smile playing at the corners of her lips, she would transport her back in time, painting vivid pictures of a bygone era filled with laughter, hardships, and triumphs.

Nya listened with engrossed attention, captivated by her grandma's tales of growing up in a simpler time, where family and community were the cornerstones of existence. Nya marveled at the resilience and strength exhibited by her grandma, who had weathered life's storms with grace and dignity. As they sat together in the cozy kitchen, surrounded by the comforting smells of home cooked meals and the gentle hum of conversation, Nya could not help but feel an overwhelming sense of gratitude for her grandma and a sense of belonging and a deep love that would stay with her forever.

Though grandma rarely uttered the words "I Love You," her love radiated from her gentle touch, her reassuring hugs, and the way she always was available to listen, no matter how busy she was. Instead, grandma's love manifested in the small everyday moments like the hearty meals she cooked. In the kitchen love was expressed through the aroma of home-cooked meals that filled the air, lovingly prepared by generations of hands passing down family recipes. In the quiet moments spent together, whether sitting on the front porch or gathered around on a chilly evening, love was present in the stories shared, the lessons taught, and the unwavering support given. The expressions of affection were often conveyed through actions rather than words, Nya learned to recognize love in the simplest yet most profound gestures of everyday life.

Although Nya understood that the word 'love' was not always spoken, she felt it in the depths of the soul. It was woven into the fabric of grandma's traditions, etched into the memories of moments both big and small. Grandma was always there and had her own way of showing love, despite the absence of verbal affection. Nya could feel it in the warmth of grandma's embrace, in the way she would stay up late into the night to comfort her when she had bad dreams. Nya had always been haunted by a recurring dream, one that started when she was very young, around three years old. It was a dream that felt so vivid, so real, that as an adult, she couldn't shake the feeling that it might have been more than just a figment of her imagination.

The night in the dream would take a dark turn. Nya would wake up in the middle of the night, startled by a strange, uncomfortable sensation. She initially thought she had wet the bed, but when she looked down at her legs and saw that they were covered in blood. It soaked through her nightgown and the sheets beneath her. Panic would set in as she tried to understand what was happening. She would scream, a shrill, terrified sound that echoed through the house. In her dream, Stella would rush into the room, her face pale with worry. She would scoop Nya up in her arms, trying to calm her down, but the blood wouldn't stop. It seemed endless, a dark, red river that stained everything it touched. Nya would cry out, begging for the nightmare to end, but the dream always ended the same way – with her waking up in her grandmother's house, safe in her own bed, but with the lingering feeling that something terrible had happened.

Nya recalled lazy Sundays when people either spent the day in church or in bed. As a child, she didn't attend church often. She would attend church with her friends sporadically. She attended bible study with the next-door neighbor Denise Johnson. Her mother was strict. Denise was not allowed to leave the porch. Nya would stay on the porch with her and play board games. Denise always had lots of board games. She had a brother who was not exactly a model citizen, so her mother clamped down on her daughter. Nya enjoyed their friendship because she learned so much when they played together. Denise never gossiped and she was never judgmental, she was like a sister Nya never had.

On Sunday mornings, Nya would get up and pour cereal and sit and watch cartoons on the black and white television. If someone knocked on the door, she didn't open it because more likely it was Jehovah Witnesses or someone who wanted to borrow a cup of sugar or an egg. Grandma, however, would rise with a sense of purpose and anticipation. Each Sunday morning, before the sun had even begun to peek over the horizon, with her hat perched just so and her Sunday best pressed and polished, she would make her way to the quaint little church at the edge of the city. The worn wooden pews and stained-glass windows, where Grandma found comfort in the familiar hymns and the comforting words of the preacher, she felt her spirit lifted and her heart renewed.

After the service, once she made her way back home, Grandma would put on her apron and turn to WVON on the radio station to listen to her gospel music. You could hear her in the kitchen humming to Mahalia Jackson while she cut up collard greens and the smell of ham hocks simmering low. The air would fill with the soul stirring melodies of gospel music, each note a testament to the power of faith and the resilience of the human spirit. Grandma would set to work in the kitchen, preparing a feast fit for a King. As she chopped, stirred, and seasoned, the music filled the air, wrapping her in a sheath of joy and gratitude. With each dish she prepared, Grandma poured her love and devotion into every spoonful, knowing that it would nourish not only the bodies but also the souls of her loved ones gathered around the table.

As the savory aromas wafted through the house, drawing her family closer with each passing minute,

Grandma would find herself lost in the music, swaying to the rhythm of the songs as she tended to the pots on the stove. And when the time came to sit down for dinner, the table would be laden with steaming dishes of fried chicken, collard greens, cornbread, and peach cobbler, a feast that spoke of love, tradition, and the blessings of the Lord. As we sat down to eat, Grandma would bless the food and the rest of us gave thanks for the bounty before us and the love that surrounded us.

Chapter 9: A Tragic Love Story

Nya would always find herself nestled at the knee of her grandma and being captivated by the stories that she would tell. Amongst the most cherished were those that spoke of love's defiance against the harsh currents of prejudice and hate.

"Child," she would begin, her voice a melodic cadence that echoed through the stillness of the night,

"Let me tell you about your other grandma Mary and grandfather Carter."

Nya would lean closer; her eyes open wide and ears eagerly excited as grandma's words transported her to another place and time.

"You know, your other grandma was a beautiful white woman," Grandma continued, her voice tinged with nostalgia.

"She grew up in a world where the color of one's skin mattered more than the goodness of their heart. But she saw beyond the barriers that society created, and she fell in love with your grandfather, a kind and gentle man with skin smooth like caramel."

"They faced many trials, my child," my grandma would say, but they stood together, hand in hand, confronting the world that sought to tear them apart."

During this time racial tensions ran high, and societal norms dictated strict segregation, but the Matthew family stood as a testament to love's defiance against prejudice. Carter Matthew, Nya's grandfather, found himself drawn to the spirited charm of Mary, her grandmother, whose laughter could light up the darkest of nights. Despite the disapproving glares and wagging tongues of their town, Carter and Mary knew that their love was stronger than the walls of bigotry established around them.

Together, they lived in a little wooden house on the outskirts of a small town, where the earth was rich, and the air was heavy with the scent of magnolias. Carter worked tirelessly in the fields, while Mary tended to their eight children with unwavering attentiveness. Their children, six girls and two boys, grew up in the warmth of their parents' love shielded from the harsh realities of the outside world as much as possible. They played in the fields, chasing fireflies beneath the starlit sky, their laughter mingling with the rustle of cotton in the breeze.

Grandma Odessa continued with the story telling Nya how tragedy struck one fateful day when the youngest daughter of the Matthew children, Little Mary, wandered too close to where Carter was cutting down a tree. The crack of splintering wood echoed through the air, followed by a deafening silence that chilled the soul. The massive oak tree, ancient and proud, came crashing down with a thunderous force, crushing everything in its path. Carter's heart shattered as he rushed to lift the heavy trunk, his hands trembling with desperation. Mary's cries pierced the stillness of the afternoon, her grief echoing the lamentations of a mother robbed of her child's laughter.

Grandma Odessa continued with story when she said it wasn't long after in the sultry heat of the summer, tragedy cast its shadow over the Matthew family once more. Not long after the loss of their youngest daughter Mary, my grandmother, Mary's health began to falter. The weight of grief bore down upon her like a heavy burden, draining the life from her weary body. Carter watched helplessly as the woman he loved, his rock and his anchor, slipped away from him with each passing day. Despite his prayers and the whispered promises of hope, fate was unyielding in its cruel verdict.

One sweltering afternoon in the field, as the cicadas sang their mournful chant and the sun beat down mercilessly upon the earth, Mary drew her final breath. Carter's heart shattered over as he held her frail body in his arms, his tears mingling with hers as they fell upon the dry earth below. With Mary's passing, Carter now faced the daunting task of raising their seven children alone. The burden weighed heavy upon his shoulders, but Carter refused to let anguish consume him. With determination, he set about the challenging task of keeping his family together, guided by the memories of his beloved wife and the promise he had made to her on her deathbed.

The Matthew children, grief-stricken, united around their father in silent solidarity. They worked alongside him in the fields, their young hands blistered and calloused from the unrelenting labor, but their spirits were unbroken. Henry had five sisters and one brother, him being the youngest of the family. They all moved from Mississippi to other various locations.

The older sister Carry Lee, who had no children, moved to Gary Indiana, along with Mable, who had three girls and two boys. Then there was Olive who had two boys and one girl who moved to Detroit Michigan. Cora and Charlotte were twins. Cora had five girls and two boys who lived in Chicago on the west side and Charlotte had four girls and two boys who stayed in Mississippi. Brother Harvey had one daughter had signed up for the Army and made a career. They all had spouses, and they all lived in nice bungalows houses. All their children were all around the same age as Nya.

Chapter 10:
Missing Pieces

Despite the absence of her father not living with her mother, Nya was surrounded by love. Grandma, a woman of strength and resilience, had raised her with unwavering devotion, filling their home with warmth and laughter, and yet, there was always a void, a missing piece of the puzzle that left her feeling incomplete. While other children talked excitedly about living at home with their moms, Nya could not relate. She would often wonder why her mother was not the one tucking her into bed at night or cheering her on at school events.

As far as Nya can remember, she had never seen her mother and father together. Her earliest memories were of her mother giving her the phone where she would listen to the distant voice on the other end. But there was always a lingering emptiness, a void that she couldn't understand. It was as if a piece of her life puzzle were missing, and she didn't know where she belonged. Nya had always wondered about him, and her curiosity only grew stronger. She would spend hours poring over old photographs, studying the face of the man she barely knew, searching for any clues that might unlock the mystery of his absence.

Nya was a bright and inquisitive child, her mind always buzzing with questions and her heart yearning for answers. Growing up without her father, she often found herself lost in a sea of wondering, who was he? Where was he? And why had he never come around? As Nya would watch other children play with their fathers at the park or share stories about their dads at school, she could not help but feel a pang of longing deep in her chest. She longed for that connection, that bond that eluded her no matter how hard she searched. But try as she might, Henry remained a distant figure, a ghostly presence hovering at the edge of her consciousness. She wondered if he ever thought of her, if he knew the ache that gnawed at her heart with each passing day.

By the time Nya turned eight, all she'd known of Henry was what she'd heard and seen in faded photographs her mother had tucked away in an old album. One sunny afternoon, as she played in the front yard, a familiar figure approached. It was her father, a tall man with a hesitant smile. Her heart raced with excitement and apprehension as she realized that this was the moment she had been waiting for. With each step closer, her nervousness melted away, replaced by an overwhelming sense of joy and anticipation. He reached out with open arms, his embrace warm and reassuring.

"Hello Nya" he would say, in his voice filled with genuine affection.

"Hello" she replied.

Nya really did not know how to respond because he was someone she really did not know.

"What you want to do today?"

"I don't know" she replied in her little, small voice.

"Do you want to go visit your cousins?"

She got excited about that idea because she didn't know she had cousins.

She hunched her shoulder to say, "I don't know."

"They want to meet you," he said.

"Okay" she replied.

That day, they drove to his sister Cora's house where Nya met her cousins for the first time, who were around the same age as she was. There was Uncle James, Anna, Bree, Bonnie, Gail, and Brooke. They would spend hours playing games and sharing secrets. In those moments, Nya felt a sense of happiness she had never experienced before. She found comfort in the laughter of her cousins and talking with her aunt and Uncle. Even though she had not experienced her parents ever being together, she discovered a new kind of family bonding with her other side of the family. There was the father, mother and the children living together as a family.

From that day on, Henry began to show up more frequently, he would arrive in his old blue and white two-tone 1964 Ford every other weekend. He was eager to make up for lost time. Nya was also excited about the visits and the adventures they would embark upon together.

Years went by; Nya cherished her weekends visiting her cousins. Uncle James was the epitome of fun and adventure. With his easy smile and infectious laughter, he was everyone's favorite uncle, always ready to whisk his daughters and niece away on exciting escapades. Uncle James had the same type of car her father had except his was green and white. The girls would pile into the two-tone ford car with anticipation bubbled within them as they embarked on the journey to the amusement park. As they pulled into the parking lot of Riverview, a kaleidoscope of colors greeted them – the whirling rides, the cheerful vendors, and the tantalizing scent of cotton candy wafting through the air. It was a playground of dreams come true, a place where laughter echoed, and memories were made.

Uncle James led the way, with them trailing behind him as they eagerly explored the wonders of the park. They raced from ride to ride, their screams of delight mingling with the sounds of the bustling crowds. Their first stop was the Ferris wheel, where they soared high above the park, taking in breathtaking views of the city skyline. Then it was off to the roller coaster, where they whooped and hollered as they raced through twists and turns at breakneck speed. But the highlight of the day was the cotton candy stand, where Uncle James treated them to fluffy clouds of sugary sweetness.

With sticky fingers and wide smiles, they devoured the sweet treat, their laughter ringing out like music in the air. As the sun began to dip below the horizon, casting a golden glow over the park, they reluctantly bid farewell to The Riverview Park. But as they piled back into the car, their hearts were full of joy and their minds danced with memories of a day filled with laughter, love, and the magic of spending time with cousins.

Chapter 11: Confused

Nya remembers when she was about nine years old. She had gotten a call from her father Henry one morning telling me that she had two baby brothers who were twins.

"Hello Nya" he began, his voice tinged with a mix of excitement and apprehension.

"I got something to tell you."

"What?" she replied.

"You have two baby brothers."

Nya's heart skipped a beat, her mind reeling with disbelief.

"You also have a little stepsister and stepbrother."

"Brothers? Stepsister and stepbrother?"

It was a revelation that stirred both curiosity and uncertainty within her.

Henry went on to explain how, he had married a woman named Lola who already had a boy and a girl, and now they have a set of twins.

"Hmm," *I thought he was still married to my mother*," Nya confoundedly thought to herself.

"They know about you, and they want to meet you," he said.

Nya mind buzzed with a whirlwind of emotions – excitement, trepidation, and a longing to unravel the mysteries of my newfound family.

"Do you want to come by and see them on the weekend"? Henry asked.

Nya wasn't sure if she was excited or confused. She thought about how all through the neighborhood and at school, all she ever heard was kids talking about their brothers and sisters. Now she could join in and tell her stories about her brothers and sister even though they didn't live in the same house.

"Yes," Nya replied.

Henry and Lola and their family lived on 16th

and Keeler in a small storefront apartment. As we approached their home, her heart pounded with anticipation. When Nya got there, the door swung open, and there they stood. Lola's son Barry was about five years old, and her daughter Jocelyn was about four years old. Jocelyn, radiating warmth and kindness; and Barry, his eyes brimming with curiosity and the twins were in the bassinette.

Lola was introduced as the stepmother, she smiled warmly. Nya heart fluttered with a mix of emotions, curiosity, and excitement.

"Hello, Nya," she said softly, her voice soft and reassuring.

"It's so nice to finally meet you."

Nya hesitated for a moment, unsure of what to say or how to feel. She had never imagined having a stepmother, and the idea was both exciting and daunting. A sense of warmth and acceptance washed over her. Despite her initial reservations, there was something comforting about Lola's presence – a sense of belonging that she had not anticipated.

As the days passed, Nya felt herself warming up to her new stepmother, opening her heart to the possibility of a deeper connection. Nya's stepmother was a beacon of light, guiding them toward a future filled with the promise of new beginnings. From that day forward, Nya and Lola formed a bond that transcended the boundaries of stepmother and stepdaughter, becoming true companions on life's wonderous journey. They bonded over Lola teaching her a few things in the kitchen and taking her to the racetrack every now and then. Through their interactions, Nya realized that Lola was not trying to replace her mother; rather she was offering her love and support.

In Lola, Nya found not just a stepmother, but a woman whose love and compassion enriched in ways she had never imagined, she felt that their bond would continue to blossom and flourish. Overtime visiting her extended family, she discovered that Lola had a passion for going to the racetrack betting on the horses. Her love for the thunderous gallops and the adrenaline rush of placing bets was something she could not resist. Lola's heart belonged to the track.

Nya often found herself torn between her desire to spend time with Lola and her interest in the chaotic atmosphere of the racetrack. Yet, Lola could not resist sharing her excitement with her, bringing her along on occasion in hopes of sparking a shared enthusiasm. On race days, Lola's excitement was intense as she carefully studied the racing forms, analyzing statistics, and discussing odds with fellow enthusiasts. Nya would observe quietly, her small hand enveloped by Lola's, the loudness of the track overwhelming my senses. Sometimes Lola's bets paid off, and she would cheer with infectious joy, enveloping Nya in her jubilant embrace. Other times, however, the outcome was less favorable, and Lola's disappointment hung heavy in the air.

Nya started to understand Lola's passion for the track. She appreciated the moments of connection they shared during the burst of activity, the laughter that echoed through the stands, and the occasional shared victory. Despite Lola's love for the racetrack, she began to realize that her place was not there. She recognized that while the track was her sanctuary, it was not necessarily Nya's. On some racetrack days, Lola would leave Nya in the comfort of their home with Henry and her siblings.

One night when Nya was visiting, Lola had gone to the racetrack. It was getting late, so Nya prepared a place for her to sleep on the green plastic sofa. The house was quiet, and the other kids had gone to bed and Henry was in the room. Nya tried to stay up and wait for Lola, but it was getting super late. Suddenly she fell asleep, awakened by something heavy on top of her and she could not breathe. She felt something strange and was confused about what it was. She tried to scream but he had his hands over her mouth. Then she heard his voice say,

"It's not gone hurt."

"Hmmm, hmmm," She murmured. Trying to scream.

She started crying and then he said,

"You better not tell nobody."

She just cried because she had no one to run to. She stayed awake until Lola came home. Nya was awake when Lola came home, but she said nothing, Nya just waited till the morning came and everybody was up eating breakfast.

Weeks had gone by, and the end of the school year drew near, and Nya wanted to stay home with grandma where she felt safe. Nya didn't want to visit her cousins or anybody. She played with her dolls and went outside and played with my friends.

Grandma's comforting hugs, the laughter shared with her uncles around the dinner table were the pillars of her security. Here, she felt understood and loved in a way that no other place could replicate. Yet, she couldn't tell her what had happened to her. Nya knew her Grandma would have taken care of the situation. Even if she had told her uncles, they would have done something. Grandma was so protected of trying to keep her from harm's way. Little did she know, harm still found its way in the place where Grandma thought would be the safest. Although, Nya and Grandma talked a lot, that was not one of the things they talked about. And television did not show things like that, especially watching The Beverly Hills Billy and Petticoat Junction.

Nya did not feel like she could tell Stella about anything because she just talked about where they were going to go shopping. Stella loved shopping and dressing Nya up in new outfits when she was around her. Nya wanted to spend time with her more doing things like going to The Riverview Park getting on rides and eating cotton candy or the movies or just seeing her perform at school. Yes, the excitement of new outfits and the anticipation of sunny adventures managed to lift her spirits momentarily. But, beneath the surface, the desire to simply stay home lingered a quiet plea in Nya's heart.

One warm afternoon, as Nya helped Grandma in the kitchen, she told her that she could tell her anything about anything. But Nya could not utter the words of what she was feeling. With a gentle smile, Grandma weathered hands cradling her hands. In her soft reassuring voice, she reminded her that she could always come to her when something is bothering her.

Months had gone by when Grandma noticed Nya hadn't been going over to visit her father.

"It's been a while since you've been over to your father's house," she said.

Nya just looked up at her, but she didn't know what to say.

"I know," she said.

"Why don't you want to go back over there?" she asked.

“I just don’t want to go back; I want to stay home.”

“What about your cousins?” she asked.

Nya thought about them, but the only way she could get there was if Henry came and picked her up and took her there.

“I don’t know,” she said.

Nya could tell her grandma knew something was wrong, but she did not know what it was. So, she did not press the issue.

Chapter 12: One Thousand Times

One morning in June 1966 Nya was getting ready for school and Diana was getting ready for work. The song "I Love you One Thousand Times" by the Platters was playing on the radio and she was singing along to the song while putting on her jacket walking out the door.

"See you later" she said.

"Okay, see you later" Nya responded.

She grabbed her purse, walked out the door and Nya continued to get ready.

Descending the steps of the building, Diana noticed a commotion at the corner of the alley adjacent to her street. Police cars with flashing lights and an ambulance stood parked, their presence casting a somber shadow over the neighborhood.

Curiosity mingled with a growing sense of unease as Diana approached the scene. She hurried her pace, her heart pounding in her chest as she feared the worst.

As she drew closer, Diana's worst fears were realized. Among the outbreak of activity, she spotted a friend of her brother with his face etched with anguish as he spoke with a police officer. Tears welled in Diana's eyes as she realized the truth – something terrible had happened, and it involved her beloved brother Raymond. With trembling hands, Diana approached the gathering, her mind racing with dread. She heard snippets of conversation – words like "shooting" and "murder" hung heavily in the air. Sending a chill down her spine.

Summoning every ounce of courage she possessed, Diana approached the friend, her voice barely a whisper as she asked the question she dreaded to confirm. With a heavy heart, the friend nodded solemnly, his eyes filled with tears. In that moment, Diana's world shattered. The news of her brother's murder struck her like a blow to the chest, leaving her reeling with grief and disbelief. Memories of happier times flooded her mind. But among the crushing weight of sorrow, clutching the friend's hand for support, she vowed to seek justice for her brother.

Diana ran back home to tell Grandma that Raymond was found in an alley shot in the head and that he was dead. She stumbled out of the alley, her brother's lifeless body etched into her memory like a haunting specter. With tears streaming down her face, she raced through the deserted streets, each step a painful reminder of the tragedy that had befallen her family. As she reached the stoop of the house, her hands trembling as she fumbled for her keys, her fingers slipping against the cold metal as she struggled to unlock the door.

Finally, the door swung open, revealing the dimly lit interior of the house where Nya was still getting ready for school. Without hesitation, she rushed inside and found Grandma in the kitchen as she was drinking her coffee, unaware of the tragedy that had unfolded just moments before. Through trembling lips, Diana relayed the devasting news. Grandma's tears mingled with Diana's as they clung to each other in their shared anguish.

Raymond was a charismatic soul with a knack for luck, particularly when it came to games of chance. His passion for shooting dice was renowned throughout the neighborhood, and he often found himself at the center of lively gatherings where Bets were placed, laughter echoed, and fortunes rose and fell with the roll of the dice. The night before, after a particularly successful streak in the alley at a local dice game, Raymond emerged from the dimly lit alley behind the neighborhood bar, his pockets jingling with winnings and a grin stretching across his face. With his friend cheering him on, he swaggered down the narrow alley, revealing the joy of victory.

But as fate would have it, Raymond jubilation was short-lived. Just as he reached the mouth of the alley, a shadowing figure emerged from the darkness, a glint of steel catching the dim light. Before Raymond could react, a shot rang out, piercing the stillness of the night. The bullet found its mark, striking Raymond in the head. The force of the impact sent him sprawling to the ground, the echoes of the gunshot fading into the night as darkness closed in around him.

In the aftermath of the chaos, Raymond's friends rushed to his side, their shots of panic piercing the night air. Among the confusion, someone called for help, and soon the sound of sirens filled the alley as emergency responders raced to the scene. Despite their best efforts, the damage was done. He was gone. As years passed, the memory of that summer night faded into annals of history, but the resilience of Raymond's spirit endured.

Chapter 13:
The Heart of Chicago

In the heart of Chicago, where the rhythm of the city pulses through the streets, there lived a legendary figure known as 'Herb Kent the Cool Gent.' Herb Kent took over the airwaves with his voice smooth as silk, his style as cool as a breeze on a sweltering summer day, and his love for music was as deep as Lake Michigan. He had become a household name in Chicago and beyond. His program was more than just a collection of songs; it was a lifeline, a beacon of culture and unity for the Black community. He had a knack for blending music with stories, weaving in tales of triumph and struggle, hope and resilience. His soulful blend that seemed to dance effortlessly through the static, bringing the latest hits and timeless classics to our little corner of the world.

At grandma's house, the rhythm of life was set to the sounds of WVON. From the moment you walked in, you could hear the familiar voices floating through the air, the radio always turned on somewhere in the house. It didn't matter where you were – in the kitchen, the living room, or even the back porch – WVON was a constant presence, like a comforting hum that filled every corner. Grandma loved her music, but she loved the connection the radio brought even more. It was her link to the world beyond the walls of her home, a way to stay informed, to feel the pulse of the city.

But it wasn't just Grandma who had a special bond with the radio. If she wasn't listening, one of Nya's uncles or her aunt Diana surely was. Herb Kent, "The Cool Gent," was a particular favorite. His smooth voice and the soulful tracks he played were the soundtrack to their lives. Even Nya, though younger, found herself drawn to the music. She didn't always understand the significance of the songs or stories behind them, but she knew they mattered. She could see it in the way her family reacted. In the way the music brought them together, even when they weren't all in the same room. The radio was more than just a device; it was a thread that connected them all, a shared experience that made Grandma's house feel like home.

Grandma, who was always in the kitchen, would often find herself humming along, swaying to the rhythm. Herb Kent's show wasn't just a program; it was a communal experience bridging the generational gap with the universal language of music. Grandma looked forward to Herb Kent's segments on the weekends, especially when he played the latest hits.

She loved his storytelling, his personal anecdotes, and his way of making each listener feel like they were part of something bigger, something cool and revolutionary. His voice was their connection to the world outside, a world filled with the sounds of Motown, rock and roll and the burgeoning civil rights movement.

Every Sunday after the gospel melodies had filled the airwaves, Herb Kent would take to the radio with his iconic show called, "Dusties After Dark." The city would tune in eagerly, waiting to be transported back in time by Herb's impeccable selection of old-school tunes and the powerful voices of legends like Otis Redding, Etta James, and Sam Cooke filled the air. With his distinct on-air style, Herb did not just play music; he painted a picture with his words. His voice wrapped around each song like a comforting hug, guiding listeners on a journey through the rich tapestry of rhythm and blues, soul, and funk.

"Good evening, ladies and gentlemen" Herb would say.

His voice dripping with charm.

"You're riding the airwaves with the Cool gent, bringing you the smoothest sounds this side of the Mississippi."

Listeners would sway to the soulful melodies, transported to a time when music spoke to the heart and soul. Herb's playlist was a treasure trove of classics, each track carefully curated to evoke nostalgia and stir emotions. As the night deepened, Herb's voice remained a constant companion to those who tuned in, His effortless banter and infectious enthusiasm turned Sundays into a celebration of music and community.

Herb Kent had a radio show on WVON. His distinct on-air style (unlike any other deejays) never shouted or screamed; he always talked in a conversational ultra cool style. Grandma would have the radio on in the background when he would end his show with a song called, "Open Our Eyes."

> "Father, open our eyes,
> that we may see,
> to follow thee.
> Lord, grant us, thy loving peace,
> And let all dissension cease.
> Let our faith each day increase, and Master – Lord, please –
> Open our eyes."

This song really became a part of Nya at an early age. The evenings just would not be right if they did not hear "Open Our Eyes." The words were so powerful. Although Herb was more than just a deejay; he was a cultural icon, a pillar of the Chicago music scene, His influence extended far beyond the confines of the radio studio, touching the lives of generations of listeners who found comfort and joy in his music.

When Dr. Martin Luther King Jr. announced plans for a pivotal Freedom Summer rally at Soldier Field in Chicago, Herb Kent knew that this was a moment that would echo through the ages. The anticipation was palpable as thousands gathered in the stadium, their hopes and dreams for equality soaring high in the summer air. As Dr. King took to the stage, his words rang out like a clarion call for justice and equality. The crowd hung on to his every word; their spirits lifted by the promise of a brighter future. But even as the rally reached its crescendo, dark clouds loomed on the horizon.

In the aftermath of Dr. Kings assassination in 1968, Chicago was a city on edge, teetering on the brink of chaos. As tensions boiled over into violence and unrest, Herb Kent found himself thrust into the role of peacemaker and healer. Herb, who was a host for Freedom Summer rally held by Martin Luther King Jr. at Soldier Field was the voice on WVON calling for calm after the Kings assassination. Blacks on the West Side rebelled in anger against the oppressive system made more apparent by the King's murder. The rioting and lotting followed with people flooding out onto the streets.

Violence sparked the West Side gradually expanding the stretch businesses along Madison Street, Garfield Park, Austin and leading to Roosevelt Road in Lawndale. As we watched the news, Grandma was praying heavily that the rioting would soon stop.

Some businesses owned by whites were looted and burned down. People died and some were wounded by police gunfire. Madison street, the place where me and my mother would shop regularly, was left in a state of rubble. Firefighters quickly flooded the neighborhoods and Chicago's off-duty firefighters were told to report to work. Mayor Daley ordered police and the National Guard into the West Side ordering "to shoot to kill" any arsonist or anyone with a Molotov cocktail in his hand and to shoot to maim or cripple anyone looting any stores in the city. Mayor Daley imposed a curfew on anyone under the age of twenty-one, he closed the streets to automobile traffic and halted the sale of guns or ammunition.

The south side had escaped the major chaos mainly because the two large street gangs, the Greystones and the Dukes cooperated to control their neighborhoods, there were gangs who did not participate in the rioting due in part to King's direct involvement with these groups. Most of the destruction was on the West Side, however there was some damage on the South Side and near North Side as far as Old Town. From the hallowed halls of WVON, Herb's voice echoed across the airwaves, a beacon of calm in a storm of anger and despair. With each word, he called for unity, for understanding, for peace. His voice carried the weight of history, a reminder of the struggles and triumphs that had brought Chicago to this moment.

"Good evening, Chicago," Herb would say.

His voice steady and reassuring.

"In times like these, we must come together as a community. We must stand strong, but we must also stand together."

His words resonated with listeners across the city, offering comfort and hope in a time of darkness. Through the power of radio, Herb Kent became a lifeline for those who sought guidance and comfort during uncertain times. And as the city slowly began to heal, Herb Kent's voice remain a constant presence, a reminder that even in the darkest of times, there's always hope. For generations of Chicagoans, his legacy would endure as a testament to the power of unity and the enduring spirit of resilience.

Even long after Herb Kent the Cool Gent left the airwaves, his legacy lived on in the hearts of those who remembered his voice, his style, and his passion for music. And on quiet Sunday nights in Chicago, when the city fell asleep to the rhythm of the past, Herb's spirit still whispers through the radio waves, reminding us of all that music never truly fades away.

Chapter 14:
Who Do You Trust?

Grandma had instilled in Nya the importance of education. She believed that with hard work and determination, she could overcome any obstacle. And so, Nya embraced her studies and aimed for excellence in everything she did. Each morning, she would navigate the chaotic streets of Kedzie Avenue, weaving between rushing cars and honking horns as she made my way to the other side. The focal point of her daily journey was the infamous place known to locals simply as the "Bucket of Blood" standing proudly at the corner of Kedzie and 16th Street.

The Tavern exuded an air of mystery and intrigue that piqued my curiosity every time she passed by. Its weathered façade, adorned with flickering neon signs and faded paint, seemed to hold countless stories within its walls. Inside, the atmosphere was thick with the scent of stale beer, cigarette smoke, and the faint whiff of trouble. The dim lighting cast long shadows on the scarred wooded floors, and the jukebox in the corner played soulful blues and jazz, the melancholic notes echoing the sentiments of many patrons.

The tavern earned its grim nickname not from any single event, but from a legacy of violence that seemed to cling to its very walls. It was a place where disputes were settled with fists and bottles rather than words, and where the night often ended in bloodshed. Despite its reputation, the Bucket of Blood had its regulars, people who found comfort in its rough edges and dark corners. People who saw the tavern through its darkest days and had somehow survived them all, the Bucket of Blood was more than just a place of violence – it was a testament to the resilience and raw spirit of the West Side.

Adjacent to the Bucket of Blood was a quaint restaurant renowned for serving the Barbeque Ribs, Rib-Tips and the best hamburgers and French fries in the entire neighborhood. The tantalizing aroma of sizzling pork and beef and crispy wafted through the air, enticing Nya's senses and tempting her taste buds with each step she took. Nya was only about eight or nine years old when she could walk home for lunch and return to school. She kept money from her allowance she got from her mother. At lunchtime, she would make her way to the restaurant, her stomach grumbling in anticipation of the delicious meal that awaited her. She would stride through the door, greeted by the warm and welcoming atmosphere that enveloped the cozy diner. Taking a seat at the counter, she would order her favorite juicy hamburger topped with all the fixings, a generous portion of golden fries, and a refreshing strawberry Nehi to wash it all down.

As she savored each delectable bite, she couldn't help but feel a sense of contentment was over her. The chaos of the city streets and the looming presence of the Bucket of Blood, this little restaurant had become her sanctuary, a place where she could momentarily escape and simply enjoy a satisfying meal in peace. With her hunger satisfied and her spirits lifted, she would bid farewell to the friendly staff and make her way back to school. Her heart was full, and her mind buzzed with the memories of yet another lunchtime adventure at her favorite restaurant.

The hallways of Howland elementary school were filled with laughter and the joyful chatter of young children. In Mrs. Thompson's fourth-grade class, Nya unwittingly became the teacher's pet. Mrs. Thompson would call on her to read a story to the class because she thought she could read so well. Nya was a bright, curious, and enthusiastic young girl with a passion for learning that was infectious. But it was not just her reading that made her stand out; it was her genuine love for school that set her apart from her peers.

Mrs. Thompson, her third-grade teacher, was a kind and nurturing woman who had been teaching for years. She had a reputation for being fair and treating all her students with love and respect. However, she could not help but be drawn to Nya's thirst for knowledge and her unwavering commitment to her studies. Nya was always the first to raise her hand in class, and she eagerly participated in every discussion. She devoured books like they were candy and would often bring interesting facts to share with her classmates. Whenever Mrs. Thompson needed help organizing materials or setting up a class project, Nya was the first to volunteer.

One day, Mrs. Thompson announced a science fair competition that would take place in the upcoming weeks. All the students were asked to choose a topic that they were enthusiastic about, conduct research, and create a presentation to share with the class. Nya eyes lit up with excitement. She had always been fascinated by space and decided to do her project on the solar system.

Over the next few weeks, Nya immersed herself in books and other resources, soaking up every detail about the planets, stars, and galaxies. She stayed up late to perfect her presentation, create a visually appealing poster, and even build a small model of the solar system. Her dedication was evident, and soon became the talk of the school. As the day of the science fair approached, her classmates were both impressed and slightly intimidated by her project. They could not help but admire her hard work and determination. However, she remained humble and always offered to help her classmates with their projects, too.

On the day of the science fair, the school's gymnasium was buzzing with excitement. Parents, teachers, and students gathered to see the presentations. Nya stood proudly beside her poster, model solar system in hand, ready to share her knowledge with anyone who would listen. Mrs. Thompson watched with a smile, proud of her dedication. Her presentation was a hit.

She explained the solar system with such clarity and enthusiasm that even the youngest children in attendance were captivated. Her classmates marveled at her model and asked questions, to which she responded with grace and confidence.

When it was time for the awards ceremony, Nya was awarded first place for her outstanding presentation. She thought to herself how she wanted her mother to share this experience with her, but she could not make it. The entire school applauded her achievement, and she received a shiny blue ribbon that she proudly displayed on her bedroom wall. But more than the ribbon, she had earned the respect and admiration of her classmates and the heartfelt appreciation of Mrs. Thompson.

Nya continued to excel in her studies at school, earning the admiration of her teachers and the respect of her peers. She was a young girl of many talents, always eager to lend a helping hand to those in need. She had a heart full of kindness and a spirit that shone brightly in her tight-knit community.

Selena and Nya met in the fourth grade in Mr. Garcia's class. As fate would have it, they lived two houses down from each other on the same street. They quickly became best friends. They were like two peas in a pod, navigating the challenges of their neighborhood together. Selena had a calm spirit and an unwavering loyalty to their friendship.

They faced each day side by side, finding comfort in their shared dreams and aspirations. Their friendship found its spotlight during school plays and talent shows, where they shared a love for music. Whenever there was a call for singing, they were the dynamic duo that stole the show. Mr. Garcia recognized their talent and encouraged their musical pursuits. He graciously allowed them to practice after school, nurturing their passion for performance.

In the echoing halls of the assembly hall, their voices intertwined in perfect harmony, captivating the audience with every note. Sometimes, just for the sheer joy of it, they would belt out Aretha Franklin's timeless classics, their voices filling the room with soulful melodies and infectious energy. Among their repertoire, one song held a special place in their hearts – "The Autumn Leaves" song by Nat King Cole.

"The falling leaves drift by the window
The Autumn leaves of red and gold
I see your lips the summer kisses.
The sun burned hands I used to hold.

Since you went away the days grow long
And soon I'll hear an old winter song.
But I miss you most of all my darling.
When Autumn leaves start to fall"

In the crisp air of fall filtering through the windows as they rehearsed, their voices rising and falling like leaves dancing in the breeze. In that song, they found comfort, joy, and a deep connection that bound them together. During their performance, they would each take solo parts, but it was when their voices merged in perfect unison that magic truly unfolded. Their friendship was a duet, harmonizing through the highs and lows of life, a melody that resonated with warmth and affection.

When there was a program that they would participate in, Nya would be so excited and wanting her mother to attend the program. But each time, she would be disappointed by the responses she would get from her.

"We're having a program this evening at school, will you come?"

"Every time I turn around you always in some kind of program." Stella would say.

"I am going to be singing on stage, and I want you to come see me."

“You need to go sit down somewhere.” Stella responded.

“Please.” Nya begged.

Stella did not come to the program. But her grandma was always there. She knew she could always count on her grandma. All the other children’s mothers were there to see their kids sing on stage.

Selena and Nya were inseparable. They would walk to school together, their laughter cutting through the city noise like a melody. They spend their afternoons at after school programs, where they participated in various programs and activities that expanded their horizons beyond the city limits. Nya loved books and fashion, while Selena found her passion in singing.

Little did they know their fathers shared a special connection that would bring them even closer together. They both lived right down the streets from each other on 16th Street. Unbeknownst to Salena, Nya had not been over there in a while. Although she missed seeing her cousins and aunt and uncle. By that time, they were in the process of moving to Gary Indiana.

Nya decided to visit Henry, hoping that things had changed, but the inappropriate touching started up again. This time Nya went completely off. She thought Lola would back her up, but she was wrong. When Henry had left and the other kids were in their rooms, Nya walked up to Lola and said,

"The last time I was here, the night you were at the racetrack, Henry did something to me."

"Did something, like what?" she asked.

Nya did not know exactly how to tell her, but she thought she would guess what she was trying to say. Nya began to try to make the words come out of her mouth.

Nya hesitated for a moment, but then she spoke up, her eyes wide with wonder.

"When I was sleeping, he......."

Lola sighed and shook her head, returning her attention to what she was doing.

"Nya, that's enough with your stories. You need to stop making things up."

"But I'm not making it up!" Nya insisted, her voice trembling. "He really did...."

"He didn't do anything, you just trying to break us up" she said in an uncaring way that Nya had never seen before. She didn't know what to say; she just wanted to go back home to Grandma.

"Nya, I don't have time for your games."

Her heart sank. Nya had hoped that Lola would believe her, and that she would protect her. But Lola's dismissal felt like a heavy weight on her chest. Fighting back tears, she turned and walked away. Over the next few weeks, she kept her encounters with Lola to herself. She didn't know what to do with what she thought they had. She learned to find comfort in her own sense of wonder and imagination.

Chapter 15:
Special Holiday

The week leading up to Christmas, Nya and her grandma would anticipate watching their favorite holiday specials on the black and white television. They would sit in front of the television and watch all the Christmas shows snuggled up together on the sofa. Grandma and Diana went out getting the final additions for Christmas day while her uncles were out hanging with their friends. When grandma and Diana came home, they would sit in the kitchen slicing and dicing stuff reminiscing. Grandma talking about the meaning of Christmas.

Nya heard grandma say, "Christmas is not like it was when I was a child. People should be thankful to be alive and be of sound mind and body." She told Diana that there were times when they were lucky to eat a full meal let alone have toys to play with. Grandma and Diana put up a tree and Nya helped decorate it and then they put lights in the windows.

Nya could never sleep on Christmas Eve. She pretended to be fast asleep in her bed while Grandma, two of my uncles and Diana would sit up and talk telling stories, cook, and eat slices of chocolate and coconut cakes and sweet potato pies that grandma said she baked for Santa Claus. Nya would pretend to use the bathroom just to see if Santa Claus had come. She saw her uncles still up assembling bikes and doll houses. She knew deep down inside that Santa Claus really did not exist and he did not bring her all those toys. On Christmas Day Nya would wake up and there would be A walking doll, Barbie doll and doll house with her car, a bicycle, and a whole lot of other presents under the tree, mostly for her. She always got what she wanted and then some. Henry had sent her a record by Aaron Neville called, *"Tell It Like It Is."* In her young mind, she had no idea why.

After playing with all her toys with Lance, grandma announced dinner was ready while Donny Hathaway's "This Christmas" played like the National Anthem throughout the house. Lance would play music by The Temptations, The Jackson 5 and James Brown while they ate, laughed, and talked. The air filled with the infectious cheer of the holiday season. All through the house, the sound of Christmas songs filled every corner, from the classics singing of Bing Crosby to the jazzy tunes of Ella Fitzgerald. The sweet melodies danced through the air, wrapping everyone in a warm blanket of festive spirit.

Outside, the streets transformed into a winter

wonderland as fluffy snowflakes gently fell from the sky, coating everything in a soft blanket of white. The glow of Christmas lights illuminated the neighborhood, casting a magical aura over the bustling city streets. In every direction, Christmas trees stood tall and proud, adorned with twinkling lights and shimmering ornaments. From traditional evergreens to modern, stylized creations, each tree was a masterpiece of holiday cheer, spreading joy to all who passed by.

Families ventured out into the snowy evening, bundled up in scarves and mittens, their faces flushed with excitement. Children laughed and played, their rosy cheeks glowing in the frosty air as they built snowmen and engaged in spirited snowball fights. Down the block, neighbors gathered, sharing laughter and good cheer as they admired each other's festive decorations. From elaborate light displays to simple, heartfelt touches, every house was a testament to the joy of the season.

As the evening wore on and the snow continued to fall, the city of Chicago was enveloped in a sense of magic and wonder. It was clear to everyone that this year, there would indeed be a white Christmas, and the spirit of the holiday was alive and thriving in every corner of the city. As the night ended, families retreated indoors to cozy up with hot cocoa and Christmas cookies, the joyful sounds of the season continued to ring out, filling the air with warmth and happiness. That old black and white television eventually gave way to a newer more modern color television. Nya and grandma continue their tradition of watching Christmas shows together every year, creating memories that would last a lifetime.

The most special holiday of all was Valentine's Day; not only was it a day dedicated to love and affection, but it was Nya's birthday - and Stella always made sure to make it extra special. On Valentine's Day morning, Nya would wake up to find a big heart shaped box of assorted chocolates waiting for her, along with a stack of brightly wrapped presents. It was a day filled with laughter, joy, and plenty of chocolates she bit trying to find the one that tasted the best until she eventually got sick to her stomach.

Nya got new outfits for every holiday of the year. As Easter approached, she eagerly awaited her new Easter outfit, carefully selected by Stella. Each year, it was a tradition for her to dress in her finest attire, as if she was going to church, even though she rarely attended services. It was simply a unique way for her to celebrate the holiday in style.

The day before Easter, Grandma would boil eggs so Nya could dye them in vibrant colors. Together they would sit at the kitchen table, dipping the eggs into bowls of swirling dye, laughing as their fingers turned shades of pink, blue and green. Nya had to go next door to Ms. Campbell's house for her to wash, press and curl her hair. Grandma or Stella did not like to do her hair because it was too long and would always get tangled. She dreaded getting her hair done. The smell of the heat from the hot comb made her stomach queasy as she sat in the chair in Ms. Campbell's kitchen. But, when she got back, grandma hid the eggs so she could find them on Easter.

On the morning of Easter Sunday, Nya would wake up to find the house filled with the sweet scent of freshly baked hot cross buns and the sound of birds chirping. But first, she had to take a trip that led her on a grand adventure through the house in search of hidden treasures.

This was one of those times when Nya went to church with the next-door neighbor's family. She wasn't sure if she went for the Lord or to show off her new clothes. The Easter basket she got would overflow with treats and treasures. Her Easter basket got bigger and more extravagant, filled with chocolate bunnies, marshmallow chicks, jellybeans, and all manner of sugary delights.

Grandma prepared to bake, dice, and fry chicken in the kitchen by herself. She usually employed Diana to do odd jobs like washing the cutting boards when she was finishing dicing and slicing and emptying the garbage. At Easter dinner, they sat down, laughed, and talked. At the end of the night when all had finished eating, there were stacks of dishes and pots and pans piled high for Diana and Stella to clean.

Chapter 16: Breaking the Cycle

Stella had always been a magnet for unhealthy relationships. It seemed that no matter how hard she tried, she found herself drawn to men who treated her poorly. Nate was one such man – a charming facade masking a dark and violent side. Their relationship starts like many others, with promises of love and devotion. But as time went on, Nate's true colors emerged. He became controlling, possessive, and eventually, physically abusive towards Stella. Despite the signs of danger, Stella found herself trapped in a cycle of fear and dependency. She believed Nate's apologies and promises would change, clinging to the hope that things would get better.

One fateful weekend, Nya came to visit. She was about thirteen years old at this time. She was lying in bed as the sun filled the room, startled by the sound of thumps and screams from her mother's room. Fear gripped her heart as she realized what was happening – Nate was again unleashing his rage upon her mother early on a Saturday morning which seemed like it was going to be a beautiful day. Determined to help her mother, she grabbed a broom from the kitchen and rushed to her mother's aid. She stood outside the door, trembling with fear and adrenaline, ready to defend her mother at all costs. But as she listened to the heated exchange between Stella and Nate, her blood ran cold. Nate was suggesting something unthinkable – he wanted to adopt her. The mere though sent shivers down her spine, and in that moment, she knew she had to escape.

Nya's heart pounded as her mother's voice filled with frustration. She had never liked Nate from the start. There was something about him that made her uneasy, something in the way he spoke to her mother, always trying to have the final word, always trying to impose his will. He never showed much interest in her anyway, which was fine by her, but today, something was different, the argument seemed to revolve around her. Nate had always struck her as being controlling and overbearing.

"I'm telling you, it's for the best!" Nate's voice was harsh, insistent.

"I would like to adopt your daughter; you need to make this official. She needs a father figure, someone who can provide for her."

"She already has a father, Nate!" Stella snapped back, her voice quivering with emotion. "And even if he's not around, that doesn't mean you can just step in and take his place. You don't get to make decisions like this without considering how she feels."

Nate's tone turned cold, almost threatening.

"You're too soft on her. She needs structure, discipline, and a real family. I'm trying to help; can't you see that?"

Stella's voice wavered, but she stood her ground. "She's not yours to control. I won't let you decide what's best for her without even asking what she wants."

There was a heavy silence that followed, and you could almost feel the tension seeping through the door. Nya held her breath, hoping, praying that her mother wouldn't give in. Finally, Stella spoke again, her voice firm but calm.

"She's my responsibility, and I will decide what's best for her. If you can't accept that, then maybe we need to rethink this relationship."

Nate's voice lowered, but it carried a dangerous edge. "You're making a big mistake. You'll regret this."

The words sent a chill down her spine. Nya

didn't want to hear any more. Quietly, she tiptoed away from the door and slipped back to the room, her mind racing. She had always sensed that Nate wasn't right for her mother but hearing him try to assert control over her life made it all too real. She was scared – scared of what might happen if her mother gave in to his demands, scared of losing the sense of safety for her and her mother.

Nya made her way back home to grandma's house, tears streaming down her face. She could not bear the thought of being adopted by a man who had caused her mother so much pain. She refused to subject herself to the same fate as Stella, trapped in a cycle of abuse and misery. When she walked in the door, she saw grandma sitting in her favorite chair. She sat down beside her and told her of the fight she had just witnessed and together they vowed to support Stella and help her break free from Nate's grip for the last time.

In the days that followed, things were tense between Stella and Nate. He became more distant, more irritable, and eventually, he stopped coming around altogether. It wasn't long before she learned that Nate was gone for good. She never talked to her mother about what she had overheard, but she noticed the change in her – how she seemed relieved, lighter somehow, as if a weight had been lifted off her shoulders.

From an early age, Nya had always been acutely

aware of the dynamics in her household. Growing up witnessing her mother endure the pain of abusive relationships, she made a silent vow to herself; she would never allow herself to fall into the same trap. Even though she had admiration for her mother and loved her, she knew that she wanted a different path for herself. Nya admired her grandma Odessa, for her strength and independence, and she aspired to emulate her.

As Nya daydreamed about her future, she pictured herself living in a modest house surrounded by a loving family like her aunts and uncles living in Gary Indiana or Detroit. She envisioned herself with a husband who treated her with respect and kindness, and two children who would grow up in a home filled with love and stability. She was determined to break the cycle of abuse whether it was physical or emotional that had plagued her family for generations. She understood that plans do not always unfold as expected, but she was resolute in her determination to create a better life for herself and her future family.

Chapter 17:
High School Days

In the heart of the vibrant South Lawndale neighborhood stood Harrison High school, a sprawling edifice that resembled more of a grand courthouse than a typical high school. Its imposing façade, adorned with intricate stonework and towering columns, cast a shadow over the bustling streets, a testament to the rich history and tradition that thrived within its walls, a beacon of learning and opportunity for the diverse community it served.

Harrison Technical High School was a public four-year high school. In the 1960's, street gangs in the area began to adopt a racial identity. The Mexican student population increased, leading to racial tension between Black and Mexican students. There were students who planned massive walkouts to fight for an end to discrimination in the school, along with other demands like more teachers of color, bilingual classes, and ethnic studies classes. By the time Nya started high school in 1971, Harrison had a diverse student population. Students attending Harrison High School came from North Lawndale neighborhood, formerly a white community that turned black in a period of ten years; South Lawndale where Harrison High School was located, gradually became a Mexican neighborhood.

It was the winter of 1971, a time when snowfall was a common occurrence, and the icy winds swept through the city with relentless force. Despite the frigid temperatures and knee-deep snowdrifts, life in Chicago continued, and schools remained open. The sight of snow-covered sidewalks and frost laden trees was nothing out of the ordinary. We had grown accustomed to braving the elements on our daily commute to school, bundled up in layers of wool and mittens, our breath forming clouds in the crisp morning air. Nya, Selena, and Annie made their way to school through Douglas Park, their footsteps muffled by the snow and their cheeks flushed pink from the cold. It was a scene repeated by students across the entire city.

Arriving at Harrison High School, they brushed the snow off their coats and stamped their feet to shake off the cold before heading inside. The halls were bustling with students, the familiar sounds of lockers slamming shut and chatter filling the air. They made their way to their respective classes. Nya's day kicked off with her gym class, that semester was swimming first period. She had to get out of the cold and dive into the swimming pool.

Despite the winter weather, the school day proceeded as usual. Teachers conducted lessons, students scribbled notes, and the rhythm of education marched on undeterred. In the classrooms, the radiators hissed and clanked, valiantly fighting against the chill seeping in through drafty windows. During lunch break, they huddled together in the cafeteria, steam rising from their cups of hot cocoa as they shared stories of snowball fights and sledding adventures. Outside, the snow continued to fall, blanketing the city in a pristine layer of white. As the final bell rang, signaling the end of the school day, they bundled up once more ready to face the wintry landscape outside. With their school bags slung over their shoulders, they trudged through the snowdrifts, their footsteps leaving behind a trail of impressions in the freshly fallen powder.

The school color was Blue and Gray, and the mascot was the "Hornets." During their time at Harrison High, they had concerts and marching bands, orchestra and ensembles and choruses. From the moment we stepped foot onto the sprawling campus, enveloped in a sense of unity and pride that transcended cultural and ethnic boundaries. Harrison High was a melting pot of diversity, reflecting the eclectic tapestry of cultures and backgrounds that defined the South Lawndale community. Within its halls of Harrison High students from all levels of society came together united by their shared pursuit of knowledge and their unwavering school spirit.

In classrooms filled with the buzz of eager minds and the hum of lively discussion. Teachers nurtured the potential of their students, guiding them along the path to academic excellence and personal achievement. From mathematics to literature, science to the arts, Harrison High offered a rich and diverse curriculum that catered to the varied interests and talents of its student body.

Outside the classroom, the spirit of the Hornets soared as students cheered on their teams at athletic events, our blue and gray colors shining brightly in the stands. Whether it was football under the Friday night lights, basketball on the hardwood courts, or track and field on the sprawling campus grounds, Harrison High's athletes exemplified the values of teamwork, dedication, and sportsmanship. During the hustle and bustle of daily life at Harrison High, friendships blossomed, and bonds made that would last a lifetime. In the cafeteria, we were from diverse backgrounds sharing meals and stories, celebrating our differences, and finding common ground in their shared experiences.

Nya walked the halls of Harrison with a sense of purpose and determination, exceling in her studies and becoming a straight-A student in math, her favorite subject. It was not just academics that made high school experience so memorable; It was the vibrant comradery of friendships, experiences, and moments that she shared with her classmates and teachers. Among them, her favorite teacher was Ms. Horne, a wise and nurturing educator who not only imparted knowledge but also instilled in her a love for learning that would last a lifetime.

One of the highlights of her high school years was her involvement in the modern dance club. Alongside her fellow dancers, she would choreograph routines and rehearse tirelessly, perfecting their moves to the rhythm of the music. Their performance during halftime at basketball games became legendary, captivating the audience with their grace and skill. One of the most beloved traditions at Harrison High was the after-school dances held in the ROTC building. Every Friday afternoon, as the final bell rang and textbooks stashed away, they eagerly made their way to the designated dance space. The air buzzed with anticipation as the first notes of slow music filled the room, and feet began to move in rhythm.

The ROTC building transformed into a vibrant dance floor, illuminated by the flickering lights and swirling colors of the ball. They all came together, united by the universal language of music and dance. From the funky soul to groovy sound beats, the playlist curated a soundtrack for their youthful escapades. The festivities did not end with the last dance step. Harrison High had a special tradition that set it apart, the joint concerts with Farragut High school. Dubbed "The Teachers Edition," these concerts brought together the musical talents of both school's educators for unforgettable performances.

The teachers, usually known for their stern demeanor in the classroom, took to the stage with instruments in hand and passion in their hearts. They belted out classic rock anthems, soulful ballads, and funky grooves, surprising them with their musical prowess. The air resonated with cheers and applause as the teachers proved that age was no barrier to rocking it out. For the students, these concerts were more than just a showcase of musical talent; they were a celebration of community and collaboration. Watching the teachers jamming on stage alongside their peers from Farragut High created bonds that transcended the classroom walls.

The Teachers Edition concerts became legendary in the annals of Harrison High's history, cherished memories that they would carry with them long after they had graduated. And as the funk era faded into the pages of history, the spirit of those Friday nights at Harrison High lived on, a testament to the power of music, friendship, and the timeless joy of coming together to dance the night away.

With determination and a strong work ethic, Nya took on the challenge of balancing school and employment, starting her first job as a Candy Striper at Schwab Rehabilitation Hospital. As a Candy Striper, her duties ranged from delivering mail to patients to providing comfort and companionship during their stay. With each smile she elicited and every conversation she shared, she found fulfillment in making a difference in the lives of others.

Nya enrolled in an Office Occupational Class offered at school. This class not only provided her with valuable skills for the workplace but also offered the opportunity to earn academic credit while getting paid. She navigated her dual roles as a student and an employee, often juggling homework assignments with her responsibilities at the hospital. Yet, despite the challenges she faced, she refused to let anything stand in the way of her dreams. Through her hard work and dedication, she excelled in both realms, earning praise from her teachers for her academic achievements and admiration from her colleagues for her professionalism and compassion. Nya ability to balance school and work served as a testament to her determination to succeed against all odds.

As Nya looked back on those formative years, she often found herself longing to relive those days, surrounded by the same people who made them so special. The laughter shared with friends in the cafeteria, the late-night study sessions fueled by determination and camaraderie, and the exhilarating rush of performing on stage, all these memories etched into her heart, timeless treasures that she holds dearly. High school was the best time of her life. And if given the chance, she would gladly go back and relive it all over again, with the same people by her side, dancing through life with unbridled passion and endless dreams.

In the heart of her junior year of high school, life threw her a curveball; She found out that she was pregnant. The news hit her hard, and she struggled to come to terms with what it would mean for her future. This was supposed to be the time of her life – the final stretch before graduation, the excitement of prom, the anticipation of what the future held. She had always envisioned herself going to college, building a career, and making a better life for herself, but now, those dreams seemed to hang in the balance.

Nya had met this young man name Terry at her part-time job at the hospital. He was charming, sweet, and seemed to genuinely care about her. It wasn't long before their relationship became serious, and in the rush of young love, she hadn't thought about the consequences. But now, staring at the positive pregnancy test, reality crashed down on her. She was going to have a baby, and she was only seventeen. Fear and uncertainty gripped her as she thought about what this meant for her future. How was I going to finish school? What would my family say? How could I, still a child myself, raise a baby? The weight of it all was overwhelming. Then she thought to herself, Stella was the same age as when she was born.

When she told Terry about the pregnancy, his initial reaction was shock. He tried to be supportive, but it was clear he was just as scared as she was. He didn't have any answers, and over time, the relationship started to strain under pressure. Nya realized that she couldn't rely on him to figure this out- she had to find her own way.

Initially she tried to hide it by wearing bigger clothes, but she knew that was not going to work for long, so she confided in her grandmother. She has always been her rock, the person she turned to in times of trouble. Her reaction was a mix of disappointment and concern, but she didn't judge her. Instead, she hugged her tightly and told her that everything would be okay, that she would get through this.

When Nya contemplated telling Stella, it wasn't just the fear of disappointing her; it was the knowledge that her pregnancy was a mirror of her own past. She replayed the conversation over and over in my mind, trying to find the right words, but nothing seemed adequate. Finally, she decided that the only way to do it was to be direct. She needed to tell her face-to-face whatever reaction she might have, and deal with it together.

With Grandma's support, Nya began to form a plan. Dropping out of school was not an option. She was determined to graduate, to create a future for herself and now her baby. It wasn't going to be easy, but she was willing to do whatever it took.

Nya spoke to her counselor, who helped set up a plan to finish her coursework. She arranged her schedule so that she could continue working part-time and attend classes, even as her pregnancy progressed.

It was exhausting, juggling school, work, and the physical demands of pregnancy, but she was determined.

As the months passed, she faced challenges that tested her resolve. There were days when she was so tired she could barely keep her eyes open in class. She focused on her future, on making sure she provided the best life possible for her child. While many would see this as a stumbling block, she saw it as a challenge that she was determined to overcome. She knew that finishing school was non-negotiable, but the looming responsibility of motherhood added an extra layer of complexity to her journey.

Nya's teachers, seeing her determination, became some of her biggest supporters. They gave her extra time to complete assignments when needed and encouraged her to keep pushing forward. They knew how important it was for her to finish school, and they admired her strength.

Terry drifted further away as the reality of parenthood set in. He wasn't ready to take on the responsibility, and eventually, the two of them parted ways. It hurt, but she knew she couldn't afford to dwell on what might have been. Her focus had to be on the life growing inside of her and the future she wanted to create. As the due date approached, she grappled with the daunting task of finding someone to care for her child while she attended school. Her gym teacher, Ms.

Montgomery, offered a solution by mentioning her aunt who lived nearby and was willing to babysit. However, Stella was not keen on the idea, citing concerns about leaving her son with a stranger.

One evening, Nya was sitting at the kitchen table with Stella, the tension between them escalated. Stella, a practical woman who had faced her own share of hardships, believed she knew the best path for Nya.

“Nya,” Stella began, her voice firm but kind, “you need to start thinking about the reality of your situation. With a baby on the way, it’s going to be impossible to manage school and work. You need to apply for public assistance and focus on taking care of yourself and the baby.” Nya looked at Stella, frustration and determination burning in her eyes. “I don’t want to rely on public assistance. I don’t want to drop out of school and just stay home waiting for a check every month. That’s not the life I want for me or my child. That’s just being lazy.”

Stella sighed, rubbing her temples. “It’s not about being lazy, Nya. It’s about being practical. Raising a child is hard work, and you need to make sure you have the support you need.” Nya shook her head. “I know it’s going to be hard, but I want to finish school. I want to show my child that no matter what happens, I can still follow my dreams. I can’t give up now.”

When the day finally came, Nya welcomed her

baby boy into the world with overwhelming love and a fierce sense of determination. Despite the challenges ahead, she was determined to give him the best life possible. Undeterred by Stella's reservations, she turned to her uncle Lance for help. Lance, who was not occupied with work at the time, stepped up to the plate without hesitation. However, Stella remained adamant that she should prioritize staying home with her own baby, failing to understand the importance of my education and my determination to break the cycle of unfulfilled potential that had plagued the family.

Despite the conflicting opinions and pressures from Stella, Nya remained resolute in her decision to finish high school. She refused to let her circumstances define her future. With each passing day, her determination grew stronger. She could not comprehend why her mother seemed to discourage her aspirations, especially when it came to education. Stella had not finished school, but she was determined to chart her own path and provide a better life for her child.

With unwavering determination, Nya juggled the demands of impending motherhood and her academic responsibility and refused to seek public assistance. She attended classes diligently, completed assignments, and prepared for exams, all while continuing working after school. As the sun set on another school year at Harrison High, and the echoes of laughter and cheers faded into the evening sky, one thing remained certain; the spirit of the Hornets would continue to soar, inspiring generations of students to dream big, work hard, and never forget the lessons learned within the hallowed halls of their beloved alma mater.

Chapter 18:
Little Did I Know

Time had passed by when Nya met Andre in 1974 working at Sears Roebuck, and their connection was initially forged by his undeniable charm and good looks. Nya was captivated by his confident demeanor and his ability to make her laugh. They had dated for a year, and Andre's charisma and promises of a bright future together made her believe in a fairy tale romance. They had gotten married with hopes of building a beautiful life together the following year.

However, once the honeymoon phase faded, Andre's true nature began to surface. The man who had once been so charming and affectionate turned into someone she barely recognized. He became increasingly irritable and critical, often lashing out at her over trivial matters. At first, it was just harsh words and cruel comments, but soon it escalated to physical confrontations. Andre's temper was unpredictable, and Nya found herself walking on eggshells, constantly afraid of triggering his wrath. She tried to believe that things would get better. She held onto the hope that the man she had fallen in love with was still there, buried beneath his anger and frustration. She suggested counseling, but Andre scoffed at the idea, refusing to acknowledge that there was a problem. As his verbal and physical abuse continued, she felt her spirit slowly breaking.

It was not just the abuse that strained their marriage. Nya discovered that Andre was unfaithful, cheating on her with another woman who happened to work at the same place they both worked. Despite his apologies and promises to change, Andre behavior only grew worse. She felt trapped in a cycle of abuse and deceit, unsure of how to escape. She had already had a son from a previous relationship and was soon pregnant with their daughter.

She remembered the time when they first met at Sears on the west side. Andre was a young man blessed with striking good looks and was quite a charmer with a smile that could light up a room. He often drew attention wherever he went. Women were naturally drawn to him, expecting his outer charm to be matched by a magnetic personality. However, beneath the surface, Andre struggled with a lack of social skills that often left him feeling isolated and misunderstood.

She was blinded by love, overlooking the signs. She reassured herself that his controlling behavior was a sign of his deep affection. But the truth was far darker. Andre's behavior grew increasingly erratic and manipulative. He would gaslight her, making her doubt her own memories and perceptions. Whenever she confronted him about his behavior, he would twist the situation, trying to make her feel like she was the one at fault. Andre's narcissism was all-consuming. He needed constant admiration and validation, and he demanded that she revolve her life around him. He would frequently belittle her achievements, making it clear that his accomplishments were far superior. If she received any attention or praise from others, Andre would become jealous and enraged, accusing her of trying to upstage him.

Andre self-esteem plummet whenever he found himself in situations that required more than just his charm and good looks. He found it challenging to connect with others on a deeper level. He was often unsure of what to say in social situations. When they would form engaging conversations with other people, Andre often found himself on the sidelines, an outsider looking in. He struggled with insecurities and a lack of direction. His downfall had taught her that she deserved better, and she refused to settle for anything less than a life filled with love, respect, and genuine happiness.

Nya sensed something was off about Andre, but she couldn't quite put her finger on it, yet there was a restlessness about him that she couldn't ignore. At first, she dismissed it as just the stress of life, but over time, the nagging feeling in the pit of her stomach grew stronger. She also saw some good things about him. He could be charming at times and hardworking and kept a steady job. He had ten siblings and was the second oldest in the family who seemed to care for his siblings and made sure his mother was taken care of. It was small things at first – late nights out with vague explanations, phone calls he'd take in another room, and an uneasiness in his eyes when she asked him about his day. He always had an answer, a reason for everything, but something didn't add up. Nya tried to push her doubts aside, telling herself that Andre was a good man; that he was just under a lot of pressure.

One evening, while Andre was at work, Nya decided to clean up the apartment. As she was tidying up, she noticed his jacket thrown over the back of a chair. Normally, she wouldn't have thought twice about it, but that day, something compelled her to check his pockets. She wasn't sure what she was looking for, but the feeling of dread was hard to ignore. When she reached into one of the pockets, her fingers brushed against something cold and metallic. She pulled out a small, crumpled-up piece of paper with an address scrawled on it. It wasn't anywhere she recognized, and the handwriting was unfamiliar. Confused and more than a little worried, she decided to investigate further.

The next day, Nya decided to go to work late and visit the address on the paper. The neighborhood was rough, a far cry from the life they were trying to build together. As she approached the building, she saw a group of men hanging around outside, their eyes following her as she drove by slowly. The tension in the air was palpable, and Nya's heart raced as she realized she was out of her element. She didn't want to confront anyone, so she kept driving, her mind racing with possibilities. Why would Andre have an address like this in his pocket? What was he doing? She couldn't shake the feeling that something was terribly wrong.

That evening, Nya confronted Andre. She tried to keep her voice steady as she asked him about the address. At first, he tried to brush it off, saying it was nothing, just a place he'd gone to help a friend. But Nya wasn't convinced. She pressed him further, her voice rising as she demanded the truth. Andre's calm demeanor began to crack. He became defensive, his words sharp and accusing. But Nya stood her ground, refusing to let him deflect. Finally, he broke down and admitted that he had been spending time with some people he knew he shouldn't be around. They were involved in things – robberies, thefts – that he had nothing to do with, or so he claimed. But as Nya listened, she realizes that Andre wasn't just a bystander; he was more involved than he was willing to admit.

Even though he had a steady job, the thrill of fast money and the dangerous allure of the streets had drawn him in. He had convinced himself that he could keep his two lives separate, that he could have his respectable job and still dabble in the darker side of life without consequences. But now, with Nya staring at him, hurt and betrayal in her eyes, he knew that illusion was shattered. Nya felt a wave of anger and sadness wash over her. She had trusted him, tried to build a life with him, but now she realized that it was all based on lies. Andre tried to apologize, to explain, but Nya wasn't sure she could ever look at him the same way again. The man she thought she knew had been living a double life, one that could have easily dragged them both down.

Nya struggled with what to do. She loved Andre, but the trust between them was broken. She knew that his involvement with those shady people was dangerous, not just for him but for her as well. The life they were building together suddenly seemed fragile, like it could crumble at any moment.

Things took a darker turn when one night, Andre did not come home. In the early hours of the morning, she received a call from the police. Andre had been arrested for armed robbery. The police had caught him in the act, and now he faced serious charges. Nya felt a strange mixture of relief and sorrow. The man she had once loved was now a criminal, and their future together was shattered. His immoral behavior finally caught up with him and the trial was swift. With a mountain of evidence against him, including his involvement in the robbery and his connections to other illegal activities, there was little chance of avoiding jail time.

Andre sat in the courtroom, his face a mask of

indifference, but inside, he was filled with regret. He had thrown everything away for the thrill of living on the edge. The judge handed down the sentence: several years in prison with the possibility of parole. As the reality of his situation sank in, Andre felt the weight of his choices bearing down on him. The friends he had on the streets, the so-called allies who had promised to have his back, were nowhere to be found. He was alone, left to face the consequences of his actions.

Being locked up was a harsh reality for Andre. The first few weeks were the hardest, adjusting to a life where his freedom was stripped away, and every move was watched. But the real challenge was the isolation – the endless hours thinking about everything he had lost.

He thought about Nya, about the life they could have had if he had chosen differently. He thought about his job, the steady paycheck, the respect he had earned before he had thrown it all away for a life of crime. Fortunately, his lawyer was able to negotiate a sentence to two years placed in a work release program due to his previously clean record and the nature of his crime. The program allowed inmates to work outside during the day and return to the jail at night, providing them with an opportunity to reintegrate into society more smoothly.

Andre kept to himself, focusing on his work, and trying to stay out of trouble. He focused on surviving, keeping his head down and doing his time. One day, while working in the kitchen, he met Officer Ricky Betts, one of the guards overseeing the work release program. Officer Betts was a fair but firm man who believed in giving people second chances. He noticed Andre's quiet demeanor and dedication to his tasks and decided to strike up a conversation.

"Hey, Andre, "Officer Betts said, leaning against the counter. "I see you're working hard. How are you holding up?"

Andre looked up, surprised by the guard's friendly tone. "I'm doing okay, sir. Just trying to get through this."

Officer Betts nodded. "That's good to hear. You know, I believe everyone deserves a chance to turn their life around. What brought you here?"

Andre hesitated but then decided to open up. "I made some bad decisions. Hanging out with the wrong crowd, and things just went downhill from there. I felt like I had no other option."

The officer listened attentively, sensing there was more to Andre's story. Over the next few weeks, they talked more, and Andre gradually shared his struggles and regrets. Officer Betts could see that Andre genuinely wanted to change.

It just so happened that Nya knew Ricky Betts; He was a young man that grew up in the same neighborhood as she did on 15th Street who happened to be their paper boy. Ricky was much older than Nya, he was more like the owner of the paper store back then. Every now and then she would run into Rickey, and he would let her know what he was into those days. He told her that he was an Officer at Cook County Jail. Nya thought that was a coincidence. She started questioning him about Andre who was incarcerated there. As they started talking, he recognized who she was talking about.

He said, "Oh I know exactly who you are talking about. He is a nice young man; he keeps to himself though."

Nya responded, "that's who I married, and he seems to have gotten himself into some trouble with some things he was doing unbeknownst to me."

"I've been talking a lot to him about getting himself on the right track, because he seems to have a good head on him, I'll keep an eye on him."

Thanks Ricky, I appreciate that," she said.

Occasionally, Ricky kept an eye on him, as promised, making sure Andre didn't get into more trouble than he was already in. Andre had completed the program after their daughter Tara was born. Nya was struck by how much he had changed; the arrogance and bravado that once defined him was gone, replaced by a quiet determination.

"Nya," Andre said, his voice filled with emotion. "I'm so sorry for everything. I'm trying to change. I know it won't make up for what I did, but I want you to know that I'm genuinely trying."

Nya looked at him, her eyes softening, "I can see that, Andre. It's good to hear you're trying. Just remember, actions speak louder than words."

Unbeknownst to Andre, Nya was grateful to Ricky for giving him a chance and whatever part he played to help him improve himself. She hoped that it would be a turning point for him, a chance to rebuild his life on a foundation of honesty and hard work. She hoped he realized he had a child to support, and he needed to be a father. And that he needed to start acting like an adult and stop doing childish things. But she also knew this was not going to work for her.

Nya had dreams of being married and having at least two kids and living in a house like the houses her aunts had when she was a kid. She did not want her kids to live like her without her mother and father being in the home. She wanted a family like on the 'Donna Reed Show' and 'My Three Sons', the shows her grandmother and she used to watch. Sometimes, though, plans don't work out the way you want. Nya filed for divorce, determined to break free from the cycle of abuse and rebuild her future. It was not easy. The memories of the good times they had shared were tainted by the pain and suffering he had caused. But she was strong, and she sought support from friends and family.

Yet, she kept it moving, figuring out what her next step would be. Growing up on the west side of Chicago, she knew the struggle intimately. Yet, when she looked into the innocent eyes of her two children, she knew she had to do everything in her power to give them a better life, with determination burning in her heart, she made the decision to move to the suburbs of Chicago, seeking a brighter future for her family. The transition was not easy. She faced countless obstacles along the way. From finding affordable housing to securing a job that could sustain her family, every step seemed like an uphill battle. But she refused to back down. She worked tirelessly, juggling multiple jobs to make ends meet, all while ensuring Mario and Tara had everything they needed.

By this time Nya was working for the government. She found herself facing the daunting task of raising her two children on her own. She had no help from her ex-husband with guidance or finance. But she refused to let adversity define her family's future. She dove headfirst into the role of sole provider for her children. She was on the go, balancing work, household responsibilities, and the needs of Mario and Tara. She found herself in a tough spot.

As a single mother raising two children on a meager twenty thousand annual salary, every dollar counted. Despite working tirelessly, she often found herself struggling to make ends meet. The weight of bills and financial obligations pressed heavily on her shoulders, with her car payments becoming a constant source of stress. One day, feeling overwhelmed and desperate, she made the difficult call to the auto company, hoping to negotiate a delay in her payments. As she spoke with a gentleman on the other end of the line, explaining my situation, she was met with unexpected kindness and empathy. He patiently listened to her concerns and offered her options to ease her burden.

In the mist of the conversation, the gentleman asked her if she attended church. Surprised by the question, she hesitated before admitting that she had not been in quite some time. Sensing an opportunity to extend a helping hand beyond financial matters, he extended a heartfelt invitation.

"If I invited you to visit my church, will you come?" he asked gently. "If you don't like it. You don't have to come back."

She felt touched by his sincerity, agreed. He provided her with the details of the church called Broadview Baptist church located in Broadview, Illinois, its location close to her workplace, and even described the color of his shirt that he would be wearing so she could recognize him. With a mix of curiosity and gratitude, she said, "Okay, see you then."

Little did she know this simple invitation would mark the beginning of a profound transformation in her life and the lives of her children. As they stepped into the church that Sunday, welcomed with open arms by a community that embraced them with warmth and acceptance. They found themselves walking into the unfamiliar church, their eyes scanning the congregation for Mr. Johnson's distinctive shirt. Spotting him, greeted with warm smiles and open arms. As the service began, she felt a sense of peace wash over her, a feeling she had not experienced in a long time. Week after week, they became regular attendees at Broadview Baptist Church.

Over time, Nya and her children found comfort and strength in their newfound faith. Mario and Tara became involved in various activities within the church, finding joy in singing in the choir and participating in youth programs. They met new friends and even discovered some old friends they already knew. And miraculously, as they immersed themselves in their spiritual journey, she noticed a shift in their circumstances.

Through the grace of God and the support of their church family, her financial burdens began to lighten. Unexpected blessings and provisions came their way, easing the strain of overdue bills and overdue payments. It was as if a divine hand was guiding them through their struggles, reminding them that they were never alone. Despite the challenges, Nya was determined to provide her children with access to quality education. She knew that the key to breaking the cycle of poverty lay in their education. So, she scoured the suburbs for the best school district, determined to give her children the opportunity to thrive.

As Mario and Tara settled into their new schools, she poured her heart and soul into supporting them. She attended parent-teacher conferences religiously, advocating for her children and ensuring they received the resources they needed to succeed. She attended every school event, cheered them on at sports games, and celebrated their achievements, big or small. Even when fatigue threatened to consume her. She pushed forward, fueled by her love for her children and her unwavering determination to give them the best probable future. Despite the odds stacked against her, her perseverance paid off. The children flourished in their unfamiliar environment, excelling academically, and forming friendships that would last a lifetime. And as she watched her children grow and thrive, she knew every sacrifice she made was worth it.

When money was tight and bills seemed endless, Nya found herself turning to her local church for support. The church was more than just a place of worship for her; it was a community that offered comfort, encouragement, and in times of need, practical help. The church's outreach programs provided food, clothing and even financial assistance for struggling families. Nya knew that asking for help was nothing to be ashamed of, especially when it came to her children's well-being.

In the embrace of faith and community, Nya and the kids found a newfound sense of belonging and hope. Their journey was far from easy, but with the grace of God and the support of newfound friends, they navigated the challenges of single parenthood together, their hearts filled with gratitude for the unexpected blessings that had transformed their lives. As the years passed, she looked back on that fateful phone call as a turning point in her life. What began as a plea for financial assistance blossomed into a journey of faith, resilience, and community. And though challenges would still arise, she faced them with newfound courage, knowing that she had a loving God and a supportive church family by her side.

Chapter 19: The Epidemic

In the 1980s there was a fear of AIDS spreading and discrimination against people living with AIDS. The nation was torn between sympathy for the afflicted and fear that the disease might spread in the general population. It was a time when misinformation was rampant, and a lot of people were gripped by fear of the unknown. Famous people like Rock Hudson died from complications related to AIDS drew public attention to the disease, as the death of tennis star Arthur Ashe who believe that he contracted the virus from a blood transfusion he received during heart surgery. Basketball great Earvin "Magic" Johnson announced that he was living with AIDS and retired from playing basketball immediately.

There were people who reacted with fear and prejudice against people with AIDS mostly because they did not want to catch it. As rumor spread the

AIDS was a "gay disease" many who were homophobic thought that this was justice. AIDS was not a gay disease; straight people also face risk of contracting AIDS. The religious and political conservatives spoke harshly about individuals with AIDS. Stories written that gay people "have declared war upon nature, and now nature is exacting an awful retribution."

When the young teenager Ryan White contracted AIDS through donated blood in Indiana due to his condition. This made him a national figure, highlighting the stigma of the disease and the misconceptions surrounding how it spread and who can contract it.

In 1986 Nya's favorite Uncle Lance had gotten sick and thought there was something wrong with his liver. Lance was admitted into Mount Sinai Hospital where he found out he was diagnosed with AIDS. The news shook her to her core. Suddenly, the vibrant world she knew seemed dimmed by the specter of his illness. Lance 's condition worsened, and she found herself unable to face the reality of his illness.

She was terrified of visiting him in the hospital, haunted by the fear of contracting the disease herself. She convinced herself that she was protecting herself, shielding herself from the pain and suffering that the possibility awaited her in that sterile hospital room. As the family wrestle with trying to figure out how exactly did he contracted the disease whether it was drugs, relationships, or a blood transfusion, they never found out how this disease carried not only a death sentence but also a heavy stigma.

Lance was always a beacon of joy and light in her world. He was the one who taught her how to ride a bike, how to dance and the one who introduced her to Jazz, who came through for her when she needed him the most so that she could finish school.

When grandma would go to visit Lance, she said that Lance kept asking about her and wanted to know why she didn't come to see him. Like everybody else she was caught in the rumors of how one can catch the virus if they were in the same room as the infected person. She wanted to see her Uncle Lance, but she was terrified. The things she heard, the whispers and rumors, made her believe that visiting him could somehow endanger her and her children. She didn't understand the disease, and her fear was compounded by the ignorance of those around her.

Grandma approached Nya the next morning. "Nya, your uncle Lance wants to see you. I know you're scared, but he keeps asking to see you."

Nya looked down, tears welling up in her eyes. "Grandma, I'm scared. I don't want to get sick and make my kids sick."

With Grandma eyes filled with a mixture of sorrow and understanding. "Nya, I understand your fear. But Lance needs our love and support now more than ever. The doctors have assured us that visiting him won't harm us if we follow their guidelines. But it's your choice, and I want you to feel comfortable."

Despite grandma's reassurances, she couldn't shake her fear. She spent days wrestling with her emotions, torn between her love for her uncle and the paralyzing fear that gripped her. Each day she hoped she would find the courage to visit him, but each day she found herself unable to take that step.

Weeks turned into months, and her avoidance only grew more pronounced. She buried herself in distractions to avoid confronting the inevitable. But deep down, she knew she was running away from something she could not escape. This was an incredibly sad time for her because during this time some funeral homes and cemeteries refused to manage the remains.

Then, that day came. Lance had passed away peacefully in his sleep, surrounded by loved ones. The regret was immediate and overwhelming. She had let her fear keep her from saying goodbye to the man who had been such an important part of her life and who had shaped her into the person she was. The man who had asked for her presence in his final days.

In the days that followed, the family gathered to mourn and remember Uncle Lance. Stories were shared, tears were shed, and she listened quietly, the weight of her regret laid heavy on her heart. She felt ashamed and guilty, wishing she could turn back time and make a different choice.

At the funeral, she stood quietly by her grandma's side, her emotions were a tumultuous storm inside her. When it was her turn to speak, she walked up to the front of the room, her hands trembling, she took a deep beath and began to speak.

"Uncle Lance was my hero," she started, her eyes filling with tears. "He taught me so much and made me feel so special. I was afraid to visit him in the hospital because I didn't understand his illness. And now I regret that I let my fear keep me from seeing him one last time. I'm so sorry, Uncle Lance."

As she spoke, she felt a gentle hand on her shoulder. It was her grandma, standing beside her, offering silent support. The room was filled with understanding nods and sympathetic gazes. She realized she wasn't alone in her fear or her regret.

In the years that followed, Nya carried the weight of her regret like a heavy burden. She missed Lance more than words could express, mourning not only his loss but also the missed opportunities to share precious moments with him. She wished she could turn back time, to muster the courage to face her fears and be there for him when he needed her the most. But as time marched on, she found comfort in the memories she shared with him. She vowed to honor his legacy by living a life with love, compassion, and bravery. And though she would always carry the regret of not being there for him in his final days, she found comfort in knowing that Lance 's spirit would forever live on in her heart.

Chapter 20:
The Challenge

Years later, after a long day of juggling work, household chores, and the endless demands of motherhood, Nya found herself feeling worn out and in need of a break. Mario and Tara were now in high school starting to take drivers Ed and wanting to drive. They also had part-time jobs after school, so she had to figure out how to get to work and come home so Mario could get to work or take his sister to work. She didn't know how they did it, but they figured it out. Life with two teenagers and only one car was a daily balancing act, but she was determined to make it work. With all three of them needing to get to various places – work for her and school for them – it required careful planning and a lot of teamwork. It wasn't easy, but they learned how to maneuver through it together.

Every day she would come home and cook and the three of them would sit down at the kitchen table and go over the schedule for the next day. Her work hours were set, but their school schedules varied with afternoon activities, part-time jobs, and homework. The challenge was finding a way to make sure everyone got to where they needed to be without anyone being late.

After leaving Andre and stepping into the role of a single mother, Nya knew she had to make some significant changes if she wanted to provide a better life for her children. She had a stable job, but the pay wasn't enough to cover all the expenses that came with raising a family on her own. She needed to do something that would increase her earning potential, and that's when she decided to go back to school and get her degree in Business Administration. The decision wasn't easy. Nya already had a full plate with work and taking care of her children. The thought of adding school to the mix was daunting, but she knew it was the right choice. She wanted to build a future where she wouldn't have to struggle to make ends meet, where she could give her children everything they deserved. And she wanted to show them that no matter the circumstances, it's never too late to chase your dreams.

Nya enrolled in a local community college's evening program. The classes were scheduled after work, which meant her days would be long and exhausting, but it was the only way she could fit school into her already packed schedule. The first weeks were overwhelming. She would wake up early and wake her children up so they could get ready for school, work a full day, attend classes in the evening, and then come home to study and take care of the household chores. By the time she got to bed, it was usually after midnight.

There were moments when Nya questioned whether she could really do it all. Balancing work, school, and motherhood was incredibly challenging, and there were times when the stress felt like too much to bear. But every time she thought about giving up, she reminded herself why she was doing it. She envisioned the future she wanted for her children – a future where they wouldn't have to worry about money, where they could focus on their education and dreams without limitations.

Since her day started early and she got off work early, she established a routine where everyone would get up a bit earlier. If they had different start times, one of them would hang out in the school library or meet up with friends before classes began. In the afternoon sometimes they would either walk or their friends' parents would give them a ride home. Mario and Tara became her biggest supporters during this time. They understood the sacrifices she was making and did their best to help around the house. They took on more responsibilities, like doing their own laundry and helping with the cooking, to give her more time to study. Their support meant everything to her, and it strengthened the bond between them.

One day as she sat at the kitchen table, sipping a

cup of coffee, her phone rang. It was her cousin, Clyde.

"Hey Nya! Long time no-see. How about we grab drinks after work tomorrow? I found this cozy little place in Schaumburg, and I think you could really use a night out. What do you say?"

She hesitated for a moment; her mind filled with thoughts of all the things she still needed to do at home and make sure Mario and Tara got to where they needed to go. But then, she glanced at her reflection in the window and saw the exhaustion etched into her features. With a sigh, she made a snap decision.

"Sounds like just what I need. Count me in!"

When the next evening came, she found herself at the quaint bar on the first floor of an office building where Clyde worked, the dim lighting and the soft murmur of voices providing a welcome respite from the chaos of her daily life. As she settled onto a barstool, a smile tugging at the corners of her mouth, she felt a sense of excitement bubbling up inside her.

As the night wore on, she found herself laughing and chatting with Clyde and his friends, the weight of her responsibilities lifting with every passing minute, and then, as if by fate, she found herself locking eyes with the man across the room. He was interested with a warm smile that reached his eyes. Clyde introduced him as Lawrence, a longtime friend of his. The conversation flowed effortlessly between them, their laughter filling the air as they exchanged stories and shared jokes.

Nya wasn't actively looking for a relationship when she met Lawrence, she thought to herself that sometimes life has a way of surprising you when you least expect it. He had a warm smile and a calm demeanor that immediately put her at ease. They struck up a conversation, and Nya quickly learned that Lawrence was an Information Management Consultant, a career that he was deeply passionate about. He had been working in the field for several years, helping businesses organize and manage their data more effectively. It was clear that he was not only good at what he did, but that he also took great pride in his work.

As they talked, Nya was impressed by Lawrence's knowledge and the way he spoke about his job. He had a steady, reassuring presence that she found comforting, especially given her own experiences with men in the past. Unlike Andre, who had always been unreliable and deceitful, Lawrence seemed genuinely honest and grounded.

As the night ended, Lawrence asked her if she liked to go out for dinner sometime. Without hesitation, she said "yes," her heart fluttering with excitement at the prospect of getting to know him better. In the weeks that followed, Nya and Lawrence embarked on a whirlwind romance, their connection deepening with each passing day. And before long, she found herself falling for this guy. Over the next few weeks, Lawrence and Nya began to see more of each other. Lawrence was always respectful and patient, understanding that Nya had been through a lot and that she was cautious about getting involved with someone new. He never rushed her or pressured her into anything, and this was something Nya deeply appreciated. He wasn't just interested in her; he was interested in her children and her life as a whole.

Lawrence's career meant that he traveled frequently, often working on large-scale projects for corporations that needed his expertise. Despite his busy schedule, he always made time for Nya. He would call her throughout the day, just to check in and see how she was doing. On weekends when he was in town, he would take Nya and her children out to dinner making sure to include them in their growing relationship. Nya was struck by how different Lawrence was from anyone she had known before. He was stable, responsible, and kind. He had his life together, and he wanted to build something meaningful with her. Lawrence also had a way of making Nya feel valued and respected, something she hadn't felt in a long time. He admired her strength and determination, often telling her how much he respected the way she had raised her children by herself.

As the semesters passed, Nya started to find her rhythm. She excelled in her classes, her hard work paid off, and she began to see the light at the end of the tunnel. She could feel herself growing more confident with each course she completed, knowing that she was building the skills and knowledge that would open doors to better opportunities. After several years of balancing work, school and family, Nya finally earned her degree in Business Administration. It was a moment of immerse pride, not just for her, but for her children as well.

They had seen her struggle and persevere, and they knew how much this accomplishment meant to her. With her degree in hand, Nya was able to apply for higher-paying jobs within the government. Her persistence and new qualifications didn't go unnoticed, and she soon started getting one promotion after another. The increased salary made a world of difference in their lives.

Soon after graduation, Lawrence and Nya stood together, hand in hand, exchanging vows in front of a judge. She could not help but marvel at the unexpected turn her life had taken. From a chance encounter at a bar to finding her soulmate, she knew that sometimes the best things in life truly did come when you least expected them. Their relationship grew stronger with time, and Lawrence eventually became a central part of Nya's life. He supported her career ambitions, encouraged her children in their endeavors, and brought a sense of peace and security that had been missing for so long. They bought a house in the western sub-burbs of Illinois, a sense of pride and excitement coursing through their veins. The spacious four-bedroom house they had built stood a testament to their journey together, a symbol of their shared dreams and aspirations.

Nya could not help but feel a wave of nostalgia wash over her. It seemed like just yesterday that she had been a single mother, struggling to make ends meet for her two children. But now, as they stepped into their new home, she marveled at how far she had come. As they began to unpack their belongings, each room slowly took shape as they put their personal touches on it. From the cozy living room where they would gather for movie nights to the spacious kitchen where she would whip up her famous homemade meals, every corner of the house radiated warmth and love.

As days turned into weeks, they settled into their new life in the sub-burbs, relishing the simple pleasures of homeownership. They spent lazy weekends exploring their new neighborhood, discovering hidden gems and local attractions. And as they watched the sunset from their backyard patio, sipping on glasses of wine, they knew they had found their own little slice of paradise.

Mario and Tara were off at college, they found themselves enjoying a newfound sense of freedom and independence. They embarked on new adventures together, traveling to far off destinations and making memories that would last a lifetime and through it all, their love for each other only grew stronger, binding them together in a bond that was unbreakable.

Life in the sub-burbs was everything they had hoped for and more. The community welcomed them with open arms, and before long, their house became a gathering place for friends and family alike. From backyard barbecues to holiday celebrations, their home was filled with laughter and joy. As the scent of grilled meats and savory delights wafted through the air, Nya waited for her grandma to arrive. When she finally arrived, her eyes widened in awe as she stepped through the threshold of her home. The grandeur of the house took her breath away, and for a moment, she stood rooted to a spot, taking in the beauty that surrounded her.

"Lord Have Mercy, Nya!" Grandma exclaimed; her voice filled with wonder. "I never thought I would live to see someone in our family living like this in such a great big house. You've done something truly remarkable, my dear."

Tears welled up in her eyes as she embraced Grandma tight, overcome with emotion at the pride and joy shining in her eyes. It had been a long journey – a journey filled with challenges, setbacks, and moments of doubt – but at that moment, she knew that every obstacle had been worth it to see the look of pride on grandma's face. As they all sat side by side, watching the fireworks illuminate the night sky in bursts of color and light, she felt an overwhelming sense of gratitude for the woman who had shaped her into the person she had become.

After everyone left for the evening Lawrence and Nya sat together on their patio, watching the world go by, Lawrence wrapped his arm around her shoulders and pulled her close. And they gazed out at the twinkling lights of their neighborhood, they knew they were exactly where they were meant to be, together, in their beautiful home in the Burbs.

When Mario and Tara left for college, the house felt quieter, emptier, and the rhythm of their daily lives had changed, they found themselves with more time to think about the next chapter of their lives. The winters in Chicago had always been a challenge – the snow, the cold, the endless shoveling. They started dreaming of a place where the sun shone year-round, where they wouldn't have to worry about icy roads or bundling up in layers just to step outside. Nya and Lawrence started planning to move somewhere West, seeking a change of weather and scenery.

So, when the idea of moving to Florida or Arizona began to take root. The more they thought about it, the more it made sense. Both states had warm climates, no snow, and with both of their jobs, they could live anywhere. Arizona was a city known for its diverse landscapes, rich cultural history, and iconic natural wonders. Even though they had taken trips to Arizona on several occasions when Lawrence was consulting and teaching, they knew a little bit about Arizona. This one time they decided to take a trip to look at houses. After several trips they finally found a house, they liked in Fountain Hills Arizona. So, they flew back to Arizona to close on the home they purchased. They were going to stay overnight and celebrate but decided to fly back to Chicago to start packing. In the early morning of September 11, 2001, they woke up to the chaotic news spreading across the nation. As they watched the horror unfolding on the TV screen, they knew their lives were about to change in ways they could not yet comprehend.

The television showed everybody in New York going on with their daily routine with the streets filled with hustle and bustle as people hurried to work. The skyline glittered under the morning sun, with the iconic Twin Towers of the World Trade Center standing tall and proud. The same, in Washington D.C., politicians and government officials prepared for another day of legislative meetings and policy discussions unaware that their lives would soon be altered forever. Then, everything changed.

A hijacked commercial airliner, American Airlines Flight 11 crashes into the North Tower of the World Trade Center, tearing through the building with a deafening roar. The world watched in horror as smoke billowed from the skyscraper, marking the beginning of a series of coordinated terrorist attacks. Within minutes, chaos descended upon New York City. As people fled the area, emergency responders rushed to the scene, their bravery shining through as they faced unimaginable danger to rescue survivors trapped in the burning towers.

As we kept our eyes on the television we saw a second hijacked plane, United Airlines Flight 175, strike the South Tower with devastating force. The impact sent shockwaves around the world, shattering the sense of security that some had taken for granted. Then in Washington another hijacked plane, American Airlines Flight 77, crashed into the Pentagon, the symbol of American military power. Passengers aboard United Airlines Flight 93 heroically fought back against their hijackers, sacrificing their lives to prevent another attack on the nation's capital.

As the day unfolded, the world watched in disbelief and anguish as the Twin Towers collapsed in a cloud of dust and debris, leaving a void in the Manhattan skyline and in the hearts of millions around the globe. The attacks claimed the lives of three thousand innocent people from over ninety countries, leaving behind a trail of devastation and loss that would be felt for generations to come.

In the aftermath of September 11th, the world came together in solidarity, offering support and condolences to the United States as it grappled with the aftermath of the deadliest terrorist attack in history. It was a day that forever changed the course of humanity, reminding us of the fragility of life and the resilience of the human spirit in the face of adversity.

In the wake of the terrorist attack, the world engulfed in a profound sense of mourning and uncertainty.

Although Nya and Lawrence had been eagerly anticipating the move to Arizona, the aftermaths of the attacks brought unforeseen delays and challenges. As the country wrestles with heightened security measures and a climate of fear, they find themselves caught in a state of limbo. The plans they had meticulously made to relocate to Arizona were suddenly put on hold as the nation focused on healing and rebuilding in the aftermath of the tragedy.

Weeks turned into months as they patiently waited for the right moment to resume their journey westward. Even with the delays and setbacks, they remained steadfast in their determination to start anew in Arizona. They spent days preparing for the move, packing their belongings, and planning because they also had sold their house.

Finally, after months of waiting, the time came for them to embark on the long-awaited journey to Arizona. As they boarded the plane bound for their new home, Nya carried a sense of resilience and hope, knowing that even in the face of adversity, she had the strength to overcome any obstacle that stood in her way. Arriving in Arizona, they were greeted by the warm desert landscape and the one hundred degrees year-round sunshine. Despite the challenges of the past months, she felt a sense of renewal and possibility as they began to build a new life in their new home.

Now it was waiting time for their furniture and cars to arrive.

Chapter 21:
Bittersweet Moment

Looking back of Uncle Calvin life when he decided, he was not going to finish school, he started hanging with some shady people in the neighborhood. Yet Calvin was very smart and intelligent young man who love to read books like '*Invisible Man*' by Richard Ellison, or *'Black Boy'* by Richard Wright. Nya always admired him because he always had a book in his hand. Calvin was involved in some incident that occurred On October 15, 1983, that made no sense at all when a young woman said she heard a gunshot, she turned and saw two men running.

The woman stated that she was quite sure that the man was the person she saw shoot the victim. She testified that she had observed the man in the community prior to the date of the shooting. She stated that she had known the victim Leonard for fifteen years. A man name Dennis testified that he had known Leonard for eight years and stated he had been friends with Calvin for six years. On the day of the shooting, Dennis, Calvin, and Leonard were in the vicinity of 16th street. They were sitting on a porch when Calvin and Leonard got into an argument and began fighting. The fight prompted by an argument concerning the money Calvin owed Leonard for juice and beans, also known as cough syrup. Leonard and Calvin exchanged words, and Leonard kicked Calvin. Suddenly, the three men went their separate ways.

Dennis and Leonard met later that evening in the vicinity of 16th Street and Christiana. They went to the Holly Restaurant and had dinner. After leaving the restaurant, Dennis and Leonard took a bus and returned to 16th street and Christiana. As Dennis and Leonard crossed the street, they heard a gunshot. They were near the alley next to the vacant lot when Dennis heard the first shot, he and Leonard began to run. Dennis said he looked back and saw Calvin standing with his arm extended and his fingers curled around what looked like a gun. As Dennis continued to run, he heard another shot, he looked back and saw Leonard on the ground in the vacant lot.

At the hospital, Leonard girlfriend accused Dennis of the shooting Leonard, and the police handcuffed him and took him to the police station. Leonard had codeine in his body at the time so that supported the notion that the argument between Calvin and Leonard arose over syrup as they were drinking on the porch. Even though gunshot residue samples were taken from his hands, he was never arrested or charged in the shooting. The police officer who testified in the case stated that Dennis informed him that Calvin was the person who shot Leonard. The Police Officer had a stop order placed on Calvin to be brought in for questioning. The Officer said he had received a phone call from an attorney who indicated that Calvin would surrender himself voluntarily. Calvin did not surrender on the date planned. However, the officer arrested Calvin.

They further stipulated that the samples were confiscated and destroyed before they were evaluated or analyzed. After the defendant's post-trial motion was denied, a sentencing hearing was conducted. Calvin was convicted of murder and sentenced to twenty-five years in the Illinois Department of Corrections. Grandma and the rest of the family was devastated after finding out That Calvin had been arrested.

Calvin's release from prison was a bittersweet moment, tainted by the injustice that had robbed him of years of his life. Seventeen long years, he had languished behind bars, and innocent man condemned by a flawed system. As he stepped out into the world once more, he carried with him the heavy burden of those lost years, a weight that no amount of freedom could fully alleviate. Despite his newfound liberty, Calvin's health had deteriorated during his time in prison. Years of neglect and inadequate medical care had taken their toll, leaving him reliant on an oxygen tank to help him breathe. Each labored breath served as a grim reminder of the toll that injustice had exacted upon his body and soul.

As Calvin reunited with his family and friends, their joy at his release was tempered by the somber reality of his condition. Grandma and the rest of them watched helplessly as he struggled to adjust to life outside the confines of prison walls, his weakened body unable to withstand the demands of everyday life. Calvin's health continued to decline despite the best efforts to care for him. The years of neglect and mistreatment had left irreversible damage, and his body was unable to recover.

As the morning sun cast its golden hues across the sky on April 2, 2002, Nya awoke to the piercing ring. Groggy and disoriented, she fumbled for her phone, her heart racing at the early hour and urgency in the ringtone. With a sense of dread settling in her chest she answered the call, her voice trembling as she spoke. On the other end of the line was her mother Stella, her words choked with sorrow as she delivered the devastating news.

"Nya," Stella's voice quivered, "it's Calvin...he's gone."

Nya heart skipped a beat, her mind struggling to comprehend the words she had just heard. Calvin was her uncle who they had grown up together as brother and sister. He was only seven years older than her. The news of his passing sent shockwaves through her, leaving her numb with grief.

Stella recounted the events of the morning, how Calvin was rushed to the hospital after suffering a seizure. Despite the frantic efforts of medical staff, he had slipped away leaving behind a void that could never be filled. As she listened to her mother's words, tears welled in her eyes; her throat constricted with sorrow. Calvin's passing felt like a cruel twist of fate, a reminder of life's fragility and the unpredictable nature of existence. Though Calvin was gone, his spirit lived in her heart, his laughter echoing in her memories she holds dear. Nya felt that he would always be with her watching over her from a place of eternal peace.

Chapter 22:
Doing the Right Thing

After Stella lost her job in the late 1990s, she decided to foster children. This unexpected surge in interest caught the attention of many, raising questions about the true motivations behind it. Was this newfound passion for fostering driven by a genuine desire to help children in need, or was it primarily about the financial incentives that came with it? One evening Stella attended a community meeting about fostering children. She had attended the meeting with a friend of hers who thought it would be a good idea. The room filled with a diverse group of people - young couples, older individuals, and even single parents – all eager to learn more about the process.

The speaker began with a heartfelt introduction. "Fostering children is one of the most rewarding experiences you can have. Thes children need love, stability, and support. It's not an easy task, but it's incredibly fulfilling." Stella listened intently to the speaker's words. She felt like she wanted to make a difference and fostering seemed like a meaningful way to do so. However, as the meeting continued, she couldn't help but notice a few comments that made her uneasy. One couple, sitting near the front, whispered to each other, "Did you hear how much the stipend is? That could really help us with our bills."

Another woman, chatting with her friends, said, "I've heard you can foster multiple children at once. Imagine the financial support from that!"

Stella decided to take the next step. She went through the rigorous application process, determined to prove her commitment. Throughout the process, she met other potential foster parents, some of whom shared genuine passion, while others seemed more focused on the financial aspect.

Over the years, she welcomed girls into her home, providing them stability and a sense of family. But despite her best efforts, each girl eventually returned to the foster care system, leaving Stella with a mixture of sadness and hope that they would find happiness elsewhere. Nya and her grandma wondered why she wanted to foster children at this time in her life, especially when she did not raise her own daughter. Nya was not sure if it were to make up for not being there for her or helping with the foster problems going on in the world.

Even though the connection between Nya and

her grandmother was unbreakable, something Nya treasured more than anything. However, her relationship with her mother Stella was different. It was complicated, filled with unspoken emotions and unresolved feelings. Nya often wished she could have had the same closeness with Stella that she shared with her grandmother. But their relationship had always been distant, strained by the circumstances of Nya's childhood. Stella loved Nya deeply, but life had been hard, and she wasn't always able to show her love in the ways that Nya needed. Even though Nya couldn't change the past, she could shape the future. She vowed to take care of Stella, to ensure that her mother lived comfortably, and to help her with whatever she needed. It was her way of showing she loved her mother, even if their relationship weren't as close as Nya had once wished it could be.

Stella, who had always been strong and independent woman, had decided to dedicate her later years to fostering children. She had a big heart, and she wanted to give other children the love and support that she sometimes struggled to provide for Nya when she was young. Then came the day when Stella opened her door to two sisters named Maya and Lily. Nya played a significant role in ensuring they lived in a safe neighborhood and attended good schools. With her help, Stella created a nurturing environment for the sisters, hoping to give them the stability they need to thrive. Nya helped Stella in every way she could. She made sure her mother's home was well-maintained, comfortable, and safe.

Stella had been fostering Maya and Lily for a year when she decided she wanted to adopt them. She never told anybody that she was going to make this move. The sisters, aged six and eight, had been through a lot in their young lives. Their mother was a drug addict who had five other children, each one placed in foster care when she could no longer care for them. Stella had taken a liking to Maya and Lily from the moment they arrived at her home. She had provided them with the stability, love, and support they desperately needed, and the thought of giving them a permanent home filled her with joy.

Stella sat at the kitchen table, carefully filling out the adoption forms. She felt a sense of excitement mixed with anxiety; the paperwork was extensive, but she was determined to complete it. As she flipped through the documents, she came across a requirement she hadn't anticipated: proof of her divorce paper from Henry. Stella and Henry had been divorced for over forty-five years. He had been remarried and had another family. But she had never received any formal documentation. She realized she needed to verify her marital status before proceeding with the adoption.

Determined to resolve the issue, Stella reached out to the county clerk's office the next day. She explained her situation to a sympathetic clerk, who promised to look into the records and get back to her. A few days later, Stella received a call that confirmed her worst fears: there was no record of her divorce from Henry.

Feeling a mix of frustration and disbelief, Stella knew she had to confront Henry. She asked Nya for his phone number and nervously dialed it. After a few rings, he answered.

"Henry, it's Stella. We need to talk, she said.

"Stella?" He sounded surprised.

"I'm trying to adopt two little girls I've been fostering. But I think we are still legally married. ... But you remarried, for goodness' sake!"

There was a pause on the other end of the line before Henry responded. "I.... I don't know, Stella. I thought we were divorced too. When I got remarried, I assumed everything was finalized."

Stella had to place an Ad in the newspaper regarding Henry Matthew to see if anyone would come forward. Since Henry or no one responded to the Ad, it was considered a done deal.

Several months later, Stella stood in a courtroom, holding Maya and Lily's hands. The judge smiled warmly at them. "Today, we are here to finalize the adoption of Maya and Lily. Stella, you have shown great dedication and love for these children. I am pleased to grant your petition for adoption."

Nya decided to buy Stella a town home out in the suburbs close to where she and her family were living. She wanted the girls to live in a good community in a good school district. Stella was in heaven living in the burbs away from the west side where the neighborhood was clean and safe.

At first, everything was going well. Maya and Lily adjusted to their new surroundings, forming a strong bond with Stella. They laughed, played, and embraced the warmth of a loving home. But as time passed, Stella noticed troubling signs in Maya, the older sister. Her behavior became increasingly defiant and unpredictable. She skipped school, lied about her whereabouts, and lashed out at Stella. Despite her patience and understanding, Maya seemed unable to overcome the trauma she had experienced before coming into Stella's care.

Stella found herself faced with a difficult decision. On one hand, she wanted to continue supporting Maya and helping her work through her issues. On the other hand, she could not ignore the impact Maya's behavior was having on Lily and the stability of their home. Despite the challenges they faced, Stella remained committed to providing a loving and supportive environment for the girls, knowing that children deserved a chance to thrive. Unbeknownst to Nya, Stella had signed adoption papers to adopt.

Maya's journey took a turbulent turn as she

entered high school. Despite Stella best efforts to provide a stable and nurturing environment, Maya's behavior began to spiral out of control. Manipulation became her coping mechanism, and she honed her skills in deceiving not only her sister Lily, but also her teachers and even Stella. At school, Maya quickly earned a reputation for her cunning ways. She manipulated her teachers with charm and fabricated stories to excuse her absences and misbehavior. With a combination of calculated lies and feigned innocence, Maya managed to evade consequences and exploit the trust of those around her.

Meanwhile, at home, Maya's manipulation targeted her younger sister. She twisted situations to her advantage, convincing Lily to cover for her lies and join her in acts of rebellion. Lily, desperate for Maya's approval and affection, became unwittingly entangled in her older sister's web of deceit. As Maya's behavior escalated, Stella found herself facing a painful reality. Despite her love for Maya, she could not ignore the destructive path Maya was on. Maya's defiance reached a breaking point, leading to her expulsion from high school and the need for alternative education.

But Maya's troubles did not stop there. She ran away from home multiple times, leaving Stella wracked with worry and uncertainty. Each time, Maya returned with a new story, weaving intricate tales to justify her actions and deflect blame. Through it all, Stella bore the burden of Maya's struggles in silence, shielding me from the chaos unfolding within her home. She could not bring herself to burden me with the painful truth of Maya's behavior, fearing it would shatter the illusion of stability she had worked so hard to maintain.

One late evening, as Nya was settling down after a long day, her phone rang. It was Stella. Nya could hear the strain in her mother's voice, even before she spoke.

"Nya, I…I don't think I can do this anymore," Stella said, her voice trembling. "I want to give the girls back."

Nya knew that taking on the responsibility of raising young children at her age had been more challenging than Stella had anticipated.

Nya took a deep breath, trying to remain calm. "Well, if it's too much, then maybe you should give them back. It's okay to admit when something is too much to handle."

There was a long pause on the other end of the line. Stella finally spoke, her voice barely above a whisper. "I can't give them back, Nya."

Confusion washed over Nya. "What do you mean you can't give them back? You're their foster parent. You can let the agency know if you can't take care of them anymore."

"That's just it," Stella said, her voice crackling. "I'm not just their foster parent anymore, Nya. I adopted them."

Nya felt a wave of shock. "You what? When? Why didn't you tell me?"

"I thought I could handle it. The girls needed stability, and I couldn't bear the thought of them being passed around from home to home. So, I made the decision to adopt them."

Nya was silent, processing the news. She had no idea her mother had taken this step.

"Why didn't you tell me before you made this decision?" Nya asked.

"I thought I could do it on my own, like I've always done. But I'm tired, Nya. I'm too old for this, and it's wearing me down. I didn't realize how much until it was too late."

Nya felt a surge of empathy for her mother. It was clear that the weight of her decision was taking its toll.

"Stella, listen to me," Nya said gently. "You don't have to do this alone. We'll figure it out together, okay? I'm here for you, and we'' find a way to make it work."

After contemplation, Nya produced a bold idea

to move Stella and the girls to North Carolina in search of a fresh start. Nya also found herself longing for a closer connection with Stella. She wanted to bridge the gap that had always existed between them; to build the kind of bond she had never had as a child. With determination and a vision for a brighter future, she set a plan in motion.

She thought it would be great not only if Stella and the girls moved to North Carolina, but Tara and the boys to move to North Carolina as well so they all could be close together as one big happy family. After all Tara's job headquarters was in Charlotte North Carolina and there would not be a problem for her transferring. Tara, being her only daughter who was the light of her life, was thrilled to start a new chapter in a new town. The thought of being close to Tara, helping her with the boys, being a part of their lives was incredibly appealing.

Nya approached Stella with her plans, assuring her that the move would provide Maya and Lily with a chance to start anew. Nya promised to take care of everything, urging Stella to simply pack her clothes and any sentimental belongings she wanted to bring along. She assured Stella that she would handle selling the house in Aurora and purchase furniture for their fresh start in North Carolina. Stella was initially hesitant, but Nya's unwavering determination and optimism eventually won her over. So, they all made the move. Finding the perfect neighborhood wasn't hard – Nya had a knack for spotting the best places.

Living close to Tara and her family brought so much joy into Nya's life. Nya sold the house she bought for Stella in Aurora Illinois using the proceeds to buy Stella a brand-new home in North Carolina. With a mixture of excitement and apprehension, Stella packed her bags, trusting in Nya's vision for her and the girl's future. The new house was spacious, with plenty of room for Maya and Lily and they didn't have to share rooms the first time.

As they all settled into their new homes in North Carolina Nya wasted no time in assisting Stella in enrolling Maya and Lily in local schools and activities, eager for them to make new friends and to embrace the opportunities that awaited them in their new community. With her guidance and support, they embarked on a journey of healing and growth, united by their shared determinations to overcome the challenges they had faced in the past. It was not long before old patterns began to resurface, and Maya's manipulative behavior once again reared its head. Maya's defiance persisted. She continued to charm her teachers and classmates, using her silver tongue to manipulate situations to her advantage. With each passing day, Stella watched with a heavy heart as Maya slipped further back into her old habits, despite the hopes for a better future.

Then, one fateful night, their newfound tranquility shattered. In the darkness, their new home in North Carolina was targeted by vandals. Maya's troubled behavior had attracted unwanted attention, and the repercussions were swift and devasting. Their house was egged, and toilet paper was strewn across the front yard and trees, leaving a mess of destruction in its wake. The incident shook Stella to its core, leaving her feeling vulnerable and exposed. Filled with a mix of anger and heartbreak, Nya surveyed the damage, knowing that Maya's actions had put her mother at risk. In the aftermath of the vandalism, Nya doubled down seeking out counseling and resources to help Stella and the girls navigate the challenges they faced.

As the holiday season approached in December 2006, Nya's family took an unexpected turn. Six months after Stella's move to her brand-new home, tragedy struck when she suffered a devastating stroke. It was December 13th, Stella was at home, waiting for the return of her great grandsons to return from school. As she stood by the door, anticipating their arrival, fate dealt a cruel blow. In a sudden and merciless twist of fate, Stella collapsed to the floor, the world spinning around her. The youngest grandson, arriving home from school, was met with a scene of confusion and fear. He frantically called his mother Tara at work, panic lacing his voice as he struggled to comprehend what had happened.

Nya received a frantic call, felt my heart lurch with dread. With trembling hands, desperation driving to get to her mother, she prayed that everything would be all right when she got to the hospital. For sixteen agonizing days, Stella remained in a coma, they gathered around her bedside, clinging to hope as they waited for signs of improvement. But despite our prayers and the tireless efforts of medical professionals, Stella's condition continued to deteriorate.

As Nya sat by her mother's bedside in the quiet hospital room, she felt a heavy weight on her heart. Stella, once vibrant and full of life, now lay motionless, her breaths shallow and labored. The doctor's words echoed in her mind, a somber reminder of the grim reality they faced. With each passing day, hope seemed to slip further away. The thought of keeping her mother on life support indefinitely felt like a betrayal of everything she stood for. Nya knew her mother's wishes well – she would not want to be kept alive artificially, clinging to a mere existence devoid of the vibrant spirit that defined her.

Nya sat there thinking about growing up, feeling there was always a part of her that yearned to spend more time with her mother. Although living with grandma, who loved her deeply and took care of her, the longing for her mother's presence was always there. Every visit from her was a special occasion, a cherished moment where she soaked up her warmth and attention. She adored her, and those brief moments together left her wishing for more.

As a child, she often imagined what it would be like with her full-time, to have her there for all the little things in life. Nya dreamed of her being there to tuck her in at night, to help her with her homework, to celebrate her achievements, and to comfort her when she was sad. But life had its own plans, and her mother's circumstances meant she couldn't always be there as much as she wanted her to be.

As she flipped through the pages of the Bible, seeking comfort and guidance in its familiar verses, a sense of calm washed over her. The words brought a sense of peace, a reminder of faith and the belief in something greater than her. In the stillness of that December day, as the rain tapped softly against the window, she felt a strange shift in the air. She looked up from the pages of the book to see her mother's chest rise and fall with less and less frequency.

With a gentle touch, she clasped her mother's hand, holding on as if to anchor her to this world for just a moment longer. Stella's breaths grew fainter until, finally, they ceased altogether. Tears streamed down her face as she whispered her final goodbyes, her heart heavy with grief yet strangely at peace. She knew that her mother was no longer suffering, no longer trapped in a body that could no longer serve her spirit. In that quiet hospital room, on the last day of the year, she said her farewell to her mother. And as she walked out into the world beyond those sterile walls, she carried with her the memories of a woman who had touched so many lives with her warmth, her laughter, and her unwavering love.

On New Year's Eve, as the world prepared to bid farewell to one year and welcome the next, Nya's world shattered once more. Stella passed away, her gentle spirit slipping away into the night, leaving behind a void that could never be filled. She found herself having a tough time being able to stay in North Carolina. She tried to carry on as if nothing had changed, but the absence was impossible to ignore. Every corner of the house, every holiday reminded her of Stella. The neighborhood that once felt so full of life now seemed quieter, and even the beautiful North Carolina scenery couldn't lift the weight of her grief.

Staying there became harder with each passing day. She found herself questioning whether this was still the right place for her. The thought of leaving crossed her mind more than once, but the idea of uprooting her family after such a significant loss felt overwhelming. She didn't want to take Tara and her boys away from the life they had started to build, but staying felt like an emotional burden she wasn't sure she could carry. At the same time, Lawrence's job wanted him to transfer to San Francisco.

The offer was flattering and came with promises of career growth, new challenges, and the allure of life in a vibrant bustling city. Moving to San Francisco felt like adding another layer of upheaval to a life already shaken by grief. Lawrence was torn. On one hand, the job offer was too good to pass up a chance to advance his career. On the other hand, he knew how much she was struggling. In the end, Lawrence decided to take the job in San Francisco, but with a condition – he would only stay there for a year. At the same time Nya had put in for a transfer to San Francisco.

Nya's hard work had paid off. She had already been promoted several times, each new role bringing more responsibility and higher pay. With each promotion, she faced new challenges, but she met them head-on with the same determination that had driven her from the beginning. As she moved up the ranks, Nya never forgot where she came from. She understood the value of perseverance and resilience, having overcome so many obstacles in her personal life. Those experiences made her even more determined to excel in her career.

She was driven not just by ambition, but by a desire to prove to herself that she could achieve greatness on her own terms. Nya's journey to success was anything but easy. While she eventually climbed the corporate ladder, the path there was filled with challenges, especially as she balanced raising her children on her own. She was offered a position as the Chief Financial Officer (CFO) for the government. It was a role she had dreamed of, one that came with a six-figure salary and the respect of her peers.

This was a great opportunity for her because she had started at the bottom, taking a job as an entry-level accountant with the government agency. The pay wasn't great, but it was a steady job with opportunities for advancement. She was meticulous in her work. Her dedication didn't go unnoticed; her boss quickly recognized her potential. She had broken through the glass ceiling, earning her place among the top executives in the organization. After staying there for a year, they found their way back to Arizona.

Chapter 23: The Meeting

After Stella's sudden death from a stroke, the once vibrant home she created fell into a disorienting silence. The girls she had adopted were now orphans and faced uncertainty once again. Without anyone to care for them, a meeting was conducted, gathering concerned parties and the adoption panel to determine the girl's fate. Although Nya was Stella's only biological child, she found herself thrust into the spotlight as a potential caregiver. However, she hesitated because her children were all grown up and the prospect of starting over with youngsters, especially troubled Maya, daunted her. She feared the weight of responsibility and worried about the legal ramifications if things went awry.

During the meeting, Nya voiced her concerns to the judge. She explained that she was not prepared to take on such a monumental task, particularly with Maya's troubled history. She felt the specter of potential failure looming over her, unsure if she could provide the stability and support the girls needed. The judge, sensing the urgency of the situation, attempted to persuade her to reconsider, emphasizing the importance of family and duty. He hinted at legal repercussions if she did not step up, suggesting that she was the next in line to care for the girls.

However, she stood her ground. After all, she'd just recently learned that Stella had adopted the girls so this news of potentially having to be their caregiver blindsided her. As the meeting unfolded, tensions ran high; the weight of the girls' uncertain future bearing down on everyone present. Her reluctance clashed with the judge's insistence, creating an atmosphere thick with uncertainty and emotion. Amidst the turmoil, the fate of the girls hung in the balance, their future uncertain until a decision could be reached.

Nya sat nervously in the room, her hands clasped tightly together as she awaited her meeting with the judge and the panel. She had done her best to help provide for the girls, but the judge's words seemed to cut deep. She could feel the tension rise. The judge, a stern-looking man with piercing eyes, wasted no time in getting to the point.

"What kind of person are you, Ms. Johnson? "The judge asked, his tone laced with hostility. "These girls have been in your family for years now, and yet you still refuse to take them in permanently. Don't you feel any responsibility towards them?"

Nya took a deep breath, steeling herself for the confrontation. She had rehearsed her response countless times in her mind, but now that the moment was here, she felt the weight of her words.

"Your Honor," Nya began, her voice steady despite the tremble in her hands, "I understand your concerns, but I must think about what's best for my family."

The judge scoffed, leaning forward on his desk, "and what exactly do you think is best for them, Ms. Johnson? Being bounced around from one foster home to another?"

Nya shook her head, her heart aching for Maya and Lily. "No, of course not. But I also must consider my own limitations, I know that if I were to take the girls in permanently, it would only be a matter of time before Maya's behavior became too much for me to handle."

The judge's eyebrows shot up in surprise. "Are you suggesting that you would mistreat Maya?"

Nya shook her head vehemently. "No, never. But Maya has done so much already, and I am afraid that my patience would wear thin if she continued to act out. I know myself, Your Honor. I know that I would punish her for her bad behavior, and I would be sitting in jail."

The judge's expression softened slightly, though the hostility still lingered in his eyes. "Ms. Johnson, I understand your concerns, but you must understand that these girls need stability. They need someone who will stick by them no matter what."

Nya nodded, her eyes glistening with unshed tears. "I know, Your Honor. And believe me, I want nothing more than to provide that stability for them. But I also must be realistic about my own limitations. I can't risk putting myself in a situation where I might be locked up."

"Ms. Johnson," the judge began, his voice cutting through the silence like a sharp blade, "I've made my decision. To ensure the welfare of the girls, I'm afraid we'll have to take possession of your mother's house and any other assets she may have and sell them off. The proceeds will go towards providing for the girls' future."

Nya's heart sank as the weight of the judge's words settled over her. She knew her mother did not own the house or anything else of significant value. In fact, it was she who had worked tirelessly to provide for Maya and Lily, sacrificing her own comforts to ensure they had a stable home and a chance of a better life.

"Your Honor," Nya spoke up, her voice trembling slightly but resolute, "with all due respect, my mother doesn't own the house or any other assets. It's all in my name. I'm the one who's been caring for Maya and Lily, and I'm the one who's been providing for them."

The judge's eyes narrowed, a hint of frustration flickering across his face. "Are you suggesting that you've been withholding this information from the court, Ms. Johnson? That you've been hiding assets to avoid your responsibilities?"

Nya shook her head, her hands gripping the edge of the table tightly. "No, Your Honor. I've never tried to deceive the court. But the truth is, there's nothing to sell. The house they lived in belongs to me and there's no other assets to speak of."

The judge's frustration boiled over into anger, his voice rising as he leaned forward in his seat. "This is unacceptable, Ms. Johnson! How dare you waste the court's time with your lies and deceit! I will not tolerate such blatant disregard for the welfare of these girls!"

Nya held her ground, her eyes meeting the judge with unwavering resolve. "I'm not lying, Your Honor. I'm telling the truth. I've done everything in my power to care for the girls, but I can't allow you to take away what little I have just to satisfy some misguided notion of justice."

The room fell silent as the judge stared at her, his anger slowly giving way to begrudging acceptance.

After a long moment, he sighed heavily and leaned back in his chair. "Very well. Ms. Johnson. I will take your statement into consideration. But mark my words, I will not rest until I'm certain that Maya and Lily are in a safe and stable environment." But please understand that time is running out for these girls. They need a permanent home, and they need it soon."

Nya nodded, her heart heavy with guilt and uncertainty. She knew that the judge was right, but she also knew that she could not ignore her own instincts. Among the attendees was Maya's teacher, Ms. Summers, whose heartfelt concern for the girls prompted her to offer temporary shelter. Her cousin, Valerie, and her daughter, Tara, attended the meeting for support.

Relieved to have a temporary solution, the girls stayed with Ms. Summers, hoping for a brief respite from the upheaval in their lives. However, their peace was short-lived. Within just two nights, chaos erupted as Maya's behavioral issues resurfaced, culminating in a distressing incident that forced Ms. Summers to call the police.

Faced with the reality of Maya's struggles, Valerie grappled with her earlier decision. She knew she had to intervene to keep the girls safe and together, especially with the state's uncertainty about providing financial support to family members who take in foster children. Determined to keep the girls within the family, Valerie stepped forward, offering to become their foster parent. Filled with hope, Valerie approached the foster/adoption office, eager to formalize her commitment to the girls. However, her optimism quickly faded when she learned about the financial constraints imposed by North Carolina's policies. Shocked and frustrated, Valerie realized that her intentions to keep the girls within the family might be thwarted by bureaucratic obstacles.

Valerie initially stepped forward to take in the girls. Nya had warned Valerie about Maya's behavior, about the challenges that came with caring for her and Lily. But she also did not want to discourage Valerie, who seemed genuinely eager to provide a loving home for the girls.

"Valerie," Nya began, her voice soft but earnest, "I need to be honest with you; Maya can be difficult at times. She's been through a lot, and it's left her with some behavioral issues."

Valerie nodded; her expression serious but determined. "I understand, Nya. But I've worked with troubled youth before. I believe I can handle whatever challenges Maya may bring."

Nya could not help but admire Valerie's confidence, but she also knew that Maya's behavior went beyond what most people were prepared to handle. "Valerie, I'm not sure you understand the extent of it. Maya can be unpredictable, sometimes even volatile. Are you sure you're ready for that?"

Valerie hesitated for a moment; her gaze fixed on her face as if searching for reassurance. Finally, she nodded. "I'm sure, Nya. I've thought long and hard about this, and I believe in my heart that I can be effective in Maya's life."

Nya sighed; her heart heavy with concern. She wanted to believe in Valerie, to believe that she could provide the stability and support that Maya and Lily so desperately needed. But she couldn't shake the feeling of dread that lingered in the pit of her stomach.

"Valerie," Nya said, "I just want you to be sure about this. Taking in Maya and Lily is a huge responsibility, and I don't want you to underestimate the challenges that come with it. "

Thank you, Nya. I appreciate your concern, I really do. But I've made up my mind, I want to do this." Valerie replied.

However, the reality of the situation quickly dawned upon her. North Carolina's rules regarding financial support for family members taking in children proved to be more complicated than she had anticipated. Desperate for a solution, Valerie turned to Henry, who was Valerie's uncle, for information about accessing Social Security benefits for the girls.

As frustration mounted, Valerie's patience wore thin. Every phone call to government agencies seemed to lead to dead ends or more red tape. The realization that she would need information from Henry only added to her exasperation. When his wife Lola intercepted her inquiries with suspicion and hostility, Valerie's frustration reached a boiling point. Lola's discovery of Henry's lingering legal ties to Stella only added another layer of complexity to the situation. As Valerie grappled with the bureaucratic maze, frustration, and resentment bubbled to the surface.

Valerie lashed out at Nya, her anger and confusion manifesting in hurtful accusations. The call came unrepetitively, disrupting her routine at work and leaving her reeling from her harsh words. Determined to understand what had transpired, she rushed to Valerie's house, hoping for clarity amidst the chaos. The tension in the air was palpable, thick with unspoken words and unresolved emotions. Her attempts to understand only seemed to fuel Valerie's anger, her frustration bubbling to the surface in a torrent of accusations and resentment. But instead of answers, Nya was met with a barrage of accusations and resentment. Valerie's anger boiled over, directed at her in a torrent of misplaced blame. Confusion and hurt clouded her thoughts as she stood in the doorway, feeling the weight of grief and frustration pressing down upon her.

"Get out," Valerie's voice was sharp, cutting through the silence like a knife. The words hung in the air, heavy with finality, as she stood frozen in disbelief. Nya had come seeking answers, hoping to bridge the gap between them, but now she found herself shut out, the door slammed shut in my face. In the end, Nya had no choice but to leave, the tension and animosity at Valerie's house too much to bear. As she stepped outside onto the cool evening air, the sting of Valerie's words lingered, a bitter reminder of the tangled web of emotions surrounding Stella's departure.

Frustration and anger boiled within her as she realized that her plans to foster the girls had crumbled in the face of Maya's volatile nature. Valerie being dumbfounded and cornered by the chaos quickly changed her mind; calling the police was a way to get rid of the girls. She reached for the phone and dialed the police, her voice trembling with a mixture of anger and resignation. The police arrived and took the girls away. She watched them get ushered into the back of the police car, their faces a mixture of confusion and fear. In that moment, Valerie grappled with a whirlwind of emotions, anger at Maya's behavior, and frustration at the system that offered no easy solutions.

Chapter 24: The System

Later Maya and Lily were placed back into the foster care system and this time taken by a military family, the Henderson's. Colonel and Mrs. Henderson welcomed them into their home with open arms, hoping to provide stability and love to Maya and Lily who had faced so much instability. Maya was a force to be reckoned with. Despite the Henderson best efforts, Maya seemed determined to push boundaries at every turn. But they held onto hope, believing that with enough love and guidance, Maya would eventually find her way.

Lily, on the other hand, was a quiet, obedient younger sister. She often found herself caught in the crossfire of Maya's antics but remained steadfast in her loyalty to her sister and her new family. As time passed, Maya's behavior began to escalate. She starts skipping school again, staying out late, and getting into fights. The Henderson's tried everything they could think of to rein her in, from strict discipline to heartfelt conversations, but nothing made a lasting impact.

Mrs. Henderson had always been curious about the past of Maya and Lily. There were gaps in their story, unanswered questions about their life before they arrived at her doorstep. Determined to fill in those gaps and ensure that Maya and Lily had everything they needed, Mrs. Henderson decided to reach out to Nya. She welcomed Mrs. Henderson into her mother's home. As they sat down to talk, Mrs. Henderson could not help but be struck by the kindness and generosity radiating from Nya.

Mrs. Henderson gently broached the subject of Maya and Lily's past, asking Nya to share whatever information she could about the girls. Nya's eyes softened with understanding as she began to recount her memories of Maya and Lily's time with her mother.

"They had been through so much before they came to my mother. My mother did her best to provide them with a safe and comfortable home with my help in purchasing them a new home and furnishing it so the girls could have their own bedrooms and decorate the way they wanted to, but we could never replace what they had lost."

Mrs. Henderson listened intently, her heart breaking for the struggles that Maya and Lily had endured. She could not help but feel a pang of guilt for the times when she had doubted the girls or questioned their behavior.

Then, Mrs. Henderson made a comment that caught Nya off guard. “If I had never met you, I would have thought you had two heads according to the stories I heard from Maya and Lily.”

Nya chuckled softly, her eyes twinkling with amusement. “Well, I suppose teenagers have a way of embellishing things, don’t they?” Nya replied. “All I ever wanted to do was to give them a comfortable, safe place to live when they were with my mother.”

Mrs. Henderson felt a wave of gratitude come over her. Despite the challenges and misunderstandings, it was clear that they were all united by a common goal, to provide Maya and Lily with the love and stability they deserved. As Mrs. Henderson left her mother’s home that day, she felt a newfound sense of connection to Maya and Lily’s past.

Then, things took a turn for the worse when Maya began stealing. It was a heartbreaking betrayal that shook the family to its core. Colonel and Mrs. Henderson realized that they could not continue to ignore Maya’s behavior or hope that it would simply go away on its own. Despite their best efforts, Maya’s behavior continued to spiral out of control, causing tension and turmoil within their once-happy household. The final straw came when Maya’s actions directly affected their own daughter. Maya had been caught stealing from their daughter's room, betraying the trust of the family who had welcomed her with open arms. It was a heartbreaking betrayal that left the Henderson's reeling with shock and disappointment.

Colonel and Mrs. Henderson knew they could not continue to ignore the impact Maya's behavior was having on their family. They made the decision to let Maya and Lily go back into the foster care system. It was a heartbreaking choice, but they knew it was the only way to ensure the well-being of their family. Lily clung to Mrs. Henderson, her own tears mingling with those of her foster mother. "Please don't give up on us," she pleaded, her voice choked with emotion. Their hearts breaking as they prepared to say goodbye. It was sad to see Lily had to suffer because of the things her sister Maya kept doing. Months after Maya and Lily left the Henderson's home, she found herself grappling with the challenges of life on her own. Despite her best efforts to stay afloat, she could not shake the feeling of betrayal that had lingered since her time with the Henderson's.

It had been a little over a year when Maya reached out to Tara because she was trying to contact Nya. She was surprised to hear from her after all this time, but she agreed to pass on the message to her. When Nya received Maya's message, she was taken aback. She had not heard from Maya or Lily in a while and often wondered what had become of them. She decided to call Maya back, thinking that she might need some money or something and she wanted to offer whatever support she could. But the conversation took a dark turn when Maya accused her of stealing her Social Security checks. Maya claimed that she was withholding the money that was rightfully theirs.

Nya was stunned by the accusations, her heart sinking at the thought that Maya believed she had betrayed them. "Maya, I don't know what you're talking about. Nya insisted, her voice trembling with emotion. "I would never do something like that to you or Lily."

But Maya was adamant, her anger and frustration boiling over. She threatened Nya, warning her to stop lying and to return the money she believed had been stolen from her. Feeling helpless and confused, Nya tried to reason with Maya, pleading with her to trust that she had no knowledge of any Social Security checks or money that belonged to her and Lily and that she would investigate to see what happened to the checks that she said they were supposed to get. But Maya refused to listen.

As the days passed, Maya's threats grew more frequent and intense. Every day Nya was getting calls with hostility and aggression from Maya or an unknown male voice on the other end of the line until she just stopped answering the calls. During her investigation, she discovered the previous foster military family, The Henderson's, were the ones who were getting the Social Security checks that Maya was talking about. Despite her efforts to understand and reconcile with Maya, she could not shake the feeling of betrayal and sadness that had settled in her heart. She wanted nothing to do with her at that point. Her only hope is that one day Maya would realize the truth and find peace within herself.

Chapter 25:
Uncovering the Truth

Grandma had been living alone in a senior citizen apartment for a long time, reveling in the simple joys of tending to her own needs and maintaining her independence and spirit. Despite her age, she refused to let anything slow her down, not even a trip to the doctor. Every few months, she would walk to her appointment at Cook County Hospital, relying on her own two feet to get her where she needed to go. The hospital was close by, but it was still a good distance from her home and getting there meant crossing several big busy streets.

Nya was always worried about navigating the traffic on her own. "I've been doing this for years. "she'd say with a wave of her hand. "I don't need anyone holding my hand." The streets she had to cross were wide and busy, full of cars rushing by without much regard for pedestrians. Still, with her head held high, she would wait patiently at the crosswalks, watching the traffic with a keen eye. She knew exactly when to step off the curb, moving with purpose and determination, her steps measured and steady.

Grandma had always been strong, self-reliant woman. She took pride in being able to take care of herself and her home, and the idea of needing help didn't sit well with her. At first, Nya admired her determination, but as the years passed, she began to worry. Grandma was getting older, and the journey to the doctor's office was becoming more taxing on her. When Nya received the news that her job was transferring her to Chicago. It felt like a full-circle moment. As the CFO working for the government, she was used to handling complex financial matters, but this transfer brought a personal connection that she hadn't anticipated.

Chicago was where her family roots ran deep and though the move was professionally driven, it also meant being closer to her grandmother, who had always been a significant part of her life. Beyond the professional challenges, her thoughts were with her grandmother. She had always been the rock of the family, but as the years went by, her health had started to decline. Nya knew that being in Chicago would allow her to ensure she got the care and attention she deserved. She didn't want to be a burden on anyone, least of all Nya, even though she knew she was more than willing to help.

When Nya brought up the idea of hiring someone to assist her with daily tasks, she resisted. "I don't need anyone coming in here, poking around my things," she would say, waving off the suggestion with a dismissive hand. "I've been taking care of myself just fine for all these years." Nya understood her reluctance. Her grandmother had always been a private person, and the thought of having a caregiver – someone she didn't know – felt like an invasion of her space. She was proud of her ability to manage on her own, and accepting help felt to her like an admission that she was losing control of her life.

Nya also knew that she needed more support than she was willing to admit. So, she took a gentle approach, emphasizing that the help wasn't about taking away her independence but rather about making sure she could continue to live the way she wanted. Nya assured her that she would find someone who would respect her privacy and understand her desire for independence. After much discussion, she finally agreed, though it was clear she was still hesitant. Balancing her demanding job with the care of her grandmother wasn't easy, but she was determined to make it work. She started by hiring a part-time caregiver who could help with her daily needs – someone who could assist with cooking, cleaning, and keeping her company when Nya couldn't be there. She arranged for doctor's visits, making sure that her health was closely monitored.

At first, grandma kept a close eye on the caregiver, supervising every task, making sure things were done her way. When Nya would visit, she would proudly show how she was still managing her daily routines, even with the caregiver's help. She would say, "I'm still running my own show here." With a twinkle in her eye, Nya knew that maintaining her independence was what kept her going.

In the evenings after work, Nya would visit her. She would bring her groceries, help with household tasks, and spend time talking with her. Those moments became the highlight of her day. Despite her age and the challenges, she faced, her grandmother was still sharp and full of stories. She would reminisce about the old days, telling her tales of her life and her family history like she used to do, and Nya cherished every word.

Nya's job was demanding, requiring precision and attention to detail, but caring for her grandmother gave her a different sense of fulfillment. It wasn't just about making sure the numbers added up; it was about ensuring that the person who had always taken care of her was now being taken care of in return. The thought of strangers in her home made her uneasy. Her home was her sanctuary, filled with memories and the comfort of familiarity, and she wasn't ready to give up control of it.

Nya made the decision along with the rest of the family to find her a doctor closer to home, someone who could provide the care and attention she deserved. Finding the right doctor for Grandma was one of her top priorities. She wanted someone who would not only be skilled in their field but also have a genuine care and concern for her grandmother's well-being. After doing some research and asking around, she found a female doctor who seemed perfect. She was highly recommended, known for her compassionate approach with elderly patients, and Nya felt a sense of relief when she finally secured an appointment.

During the first few visits, this doctor seemed to be exactly what grandma needed. Her name was Dr. Patel, who had a warm smile and a reassuring demeanor, and she promised to take good care of grandma. She was warm and personable, taking the time to listen to her concerns and answering her questions with patience and understanding. She didn't rush through appointments, making sure her grandma felt heard and valued. She appreciated how she treated her grandma with respect, explaining things clearly and ensuring that her grandma understood her health situation.

Grandma seemed to warm up to her as well. She liked the fact that Dr. Patel took the time to get to know her, not just as a patient, but as a person. Dr. Patel asked about her life, her family, and her daily routines, and seemed genuinely interested in helping her maintain her independence for as long as possible. Nya felt reassured, thinking she had found someone who truly had her grandmother's' best interest at heart.

But as time went on, Nya noticed small things that didn't sit right with her. Dr. Patel started recommending more tests and treatments that seemed unnecessary. She would prescribe new medications without fully explaining why, and when Nya asked questions, her answers became more vague and less reassuring. There was a subtle shift in her demeanor – where once she had been attentive and caring, she now seemed more focused on getting through the appointment quickly.

Nya noticed her grandmother, who had initially trusted the doctor, was starting to feel uneasy. She mentioned that the doctor seemed distracted during their visits, no longer asking about her life, or listening to her concerns with the same level of interest. Grandma's health wasn't improving the way she had hoped, and she began to wonder if the doctor was really paying attention to what was best for her.

Then, one day, Nya overheard a conversation between the doctor and another patient in the waiting room. They were discussing a treatment plan that sounded suspiciously like what had been recommended for her grandmother. The patient expressed concerns about the cost, and the doctor brushed it off, saying, "it's just the standard protocol. The more tests we do, the better."

A sinking feeling settled in her stomach. It started to become clear that the doctor might not be as focused on her grandmother's best interest as she had initially seemed. She was more concerned with following a formulaic approach, or worse, maximizing profits through unnecessary tests and treatments. Nya couldn't shake the feeling that something was not right. It didn't take long for her to realize that this doctor also had a different attitude towards other older patients.

Instead of listening to grandma's concerns and addressing her health issues, Dr. Patel seemed dismissive, attributing everything to old age and offering little in the way of solutions and prescribing medications that she didn't need. It was as if she saw grandma as just another elderly patient, rather than the vibrant woman she truly was. Nya decided to confront the doctor during the next appointment, asking her directly about the necessity of the treatments and medications. Her response was defensive, and she avoided her questions, insisting that everything she had recommended was for her grandmother's benefit. But her explanations felt hollow, and the trust she had initially felt began to erode.

Nya regretted the day she brought grandma to see Dr. Patel. With each visit, her health seemed to deteriorate further, and she couldn't shake the feeling that this doctor was contributing to her decline. But by then, it was too late to change course. But as time passed and age began to take its toll, Grandma once unwavering health began to falter. Nya noticed a change in grandma's health. She seemed more tired, frail, and her once vibrant energy began to wane. Grandma was admitted into the hospital, and they could not figure out what exactly was wrong. They ran tests on her but found nothing. The doctors attributed her failing health was due to old age. Nya found that hard to believe, because she walked into Dr. Patel's office as a vibrant woman with lots of energy for a ninety-year-old and never walk out the same way.

The signs were subtle at first, a slight tremor in her hands, moments of forgetfulness that she brushed off with a laugh. But soon, it became clear that grandma needed more help than she was willing to admit. They watched with growing concern as her health declined, knowing that the time had come to make a difficult decision. Reluctantly, Nya broached the subject of moving grandma into a nursing home. They knew it would not be easy; Grandma cherished her independence more than anything else, and the idea of relinquishing control was unthinkable for her. But her declining health left them with no choice but to intervene.

As the family sat down to discuss the matter with Grandma, emotions ran high. Tears welled in her eyes as she listened to their concerns, her heart heavy with the realization that her days of living on her own were numbered. Despite their reassurances and promises of better care in a nursing home, Grandma could not shake the feeling of loss that consumed her.

In the days leading up to the move, Grandma grappled with a mixture of fear and resentment. She resented her failing health for robbing her of the independence she had fought so hard to maintain. She feared the unknown, dreading the thought of being confined to a nursing home, surrounded by strangers.

As the day of the move arrived, Grandma's heart was heavy with uncertainty, but also with gratitude for the family who stood by her side. With tear-filled eyes, she bid farewell to her beloved apartment, knowing that the road ahead would be difficult, but trusting that she would not have to walk alone. And as she settled into her new home in the nursing facility, surrounded by unfamiliar faces but buoyed by the love of her family, Grandma tried to find comfort in the knowledge that, no matter what challenges lay ahead, she would face them with the strength and resilience that had always defined her.

The nursing home seemed like a foreign landscape to Nya as she made her way through the sterile corridors towards grandma's room. The antiseptic smell hung heavy in the air, mingling with the hushed whispers of the residents and the distant hum of medical equipment. As Nya entered the room, her heart sank at the sight before her. Grandma, once vibrant and strong, now appeared frail and despondent, her eyes clouded with sadness. Nya's stomach churned with unease as she noticed the bruise on grandma's wrist, a stark contrast against her pale skin.

"Grandma, what happened?" Nya asked, her voice tinged with concern as she gently reached for her hand. But grandma's response sent a shiver down her spine.

"Why did you do this me?" Grandma's voice was barely a whisper, but the accusation rang loud in the air, leaving Nya reeling in confusion and guilt.

Frozen in shock, Nya struggled to find the words to respond. She searched her grandma's eyes for answers, but all she found was a silent plea for escape from the confines of the nursing home. In that moment, her heart broke for her grandma, trapped in a place where she felt powerless and alone. The question hit Nya like a punch to the gut. She hadn't expected this, hadn't prepared herself for the possibility that Grandma might feel abandoned or betrayed. Grandma's eyes, once so full of life and wisdom, were now clouded with confusion. She didn't seem to understand, or maybe she didn't want to. The hurt in her expression was unmistakable, and it tore Nya apart to see it.

"Why did you leave me here?" Grandma whispered; her voice barely audible. "I don't know these people, Nya. I don't want to be here."

Nya felt tears welling up in her eyes, but she blinked them back, trying to stay strong for Grandma's sake.

" I know it's not what you wanted, Grandma," she said, her voice trembling. "But I couldn't take care of you by myself. I didn't want anything to happen to you. I thought.... I thought this was the best way to keep you safe."

But even as she said the words, Nya knew they weren't enough. How could they be? She had taken the one person who had always been there for her, who had always protected her, and placed her in a situation that made her feel vulnerable and alone.

Grandma turned her head away, closing her eyes as if she couldn't bear to look at Nya. "I just want to go home," she whispered, her voice breaking.

"I'm so sorry, Grandma," Nya whispered, tears streaming down her face. "I'm so, so sorry."

The weight of guilt pressed down upon her, fueled by the haunting words that echoed in her mind long after she left Grandma's room.

Determined to uncover the truth, Nya embarked on a quest for answers, delving into the depths of the nursing home's practices and policies. What she discovered was a web of neglect and mistreatment, hidden beneath a façade of false assurances and empty promises. With a fire ignited with her, she vowed to fight for her grandma's dignity and well-being. Armed with determination and unwavering resolve, she confronted the nursing home administration, demanding accountability for the harm inflicted upon her grandma and countless others.

About a year and a half had passed, Nya carried the memory of Grandma's accusation with her, a constant reminder of the importance of speaking up for those who cannot speak for themselves and fighting for the right s and dignity of every individual, no matter their age or circumstance. Soon after, Nya transferred to Asheville, North Carolina, for her job. She'd just arrived days earlier when she got a phone call that shattered her world. The news hit her like a sledgehammer to the chest; her beloved grandmother, her mother figure, had passed away.

Tears streamed down her face as she struggled to comprehend the enormity of the loss. How could she reconcile the gaping void left by the woman who had shaped her life, who had been her rock through every storm? In her stricken haze, her mind raced with thoughts of home, of the familiar comforts of her grandma embrace. She longed to be there, to say goodbye, to honor the woman who had given her everything. But distance stood as an insurmountable barrier, trapping her in a city that suddenly felt foreign and unwelcoming.

Desperate to attend Grandma's funeral, she

reached out to a cousin, pleading for a few more days before they planned the funeral so that she could say her final goodbyes. But her pleas were ignored, as the cousin, consumed by her own grief and responsibilities, forged ahead with the funeral arrangements, leaving her to grapple with the bitter sting of abandonment.

In the days that followed, her grief morphed into a turbulent mix of anger and sorrow. How could her family betray her in her hour of need? How could they disregard her wishes and deny her the chance to bid farewell to the woman who had meant everything to her? As the funeral date approached, Nya found herself adrift in a sea of conflicting emotions, her heart torn between the need for closure and the betrayal that gnawed at her soul. And on the day of her grandma's funeral, as she sat alone in her apartment, thousands of miles away, she made a silent vow to honor her grandma's memory in her own way, by living a life guided by the lessons of love, resilience, and strength that she had imparted upon her.

Although Nya may have been denied the chance to say goodbye in person, she carried her grandma's spirit with her, a guiding light that illuminated the darkest corners of her grief-stricken heart. In the years that followed, as she navigated the trials and tribulations of life, she found comfort in the memories of her grandma, her guiding star in a world that often felt cold and unforgiving.

Chapter 26:
A Heavy Burden Lifted

Nya could remember as a youngster visiting her father's house; she looked forward to watching Lola make banana pudding, the dessert her father Henry loved more than anything. She had a way of making even the simplest tasks look like an art form, and she was captivated by her every move. She watched her peel the bananas, slicing each one with precision and arranging the slices in a neat layer at the bottom of a large bowl. She watched her make the custard. This part always fascinated her. Once the custard was ready, she pored over the sliced bananas, then added another layer of vanilla wafers on top. The process was repeated until the bowl was full.

It had been a while since she spoke to them. Nya got a call from Barry who told her that Lola decided to make her famous banana pudding after dinner. She imagined Henry being a huge fan, dug into his bowl, savoring each spoonful. Barry said as he reached the halfway point, he did not feel right. A sharp pain twisted in his stomach, and he suddenly felt nauseous. Ignoring the discomfort at first, he continued to eat, hoping it was just a passing sensation.

However, the feeling only intensified, and before he knew it, he was rushing to the bathroom, doubled over in pain. Violent waves of nausea overtook him, and he began vomiting uncontrollably. Panic set in as he saw streaks of blood mingling with the contents of his stomach. Lola, alarmed by the commotion, rushed to Henry's side, her heart pounding with fear. She called for an ambulance, and soon Henry was on his way to the hospital, squirming in agony. At the hospital, doctors ran a battery of tests, trying to determine the cause of Henry's sudden illness. After what felt like an eternity of waiting, the results came back, revealing a shocking diagnosis.

Henry had torn his esophagus from coughing violently, which had caused stomach acid to leak into his body, leading to excruciating pain and internal bleeding. The doctor explained that this condition, known as a Mallory-Weiss tear, required immediate medical attention. Lola felt a wave of guilt wash over her as she realized that Henry's illness might have been triggered by her rich and creamy banana pudding. She blamed herself for his suffering, wishing she had been more attentive to his discomfort earlier.

As Henry underwent treatment to repair the tear in his esophagus, Lola stayed faithfully by his side, vowing to be more cautious in the future. There was a glimmer of hope that he would recover. We all held onto that hope tightly, praying for his full recovery with every passing day. However, as time went on, it became evident that something was still very wrong. Henry's condition did not improve as expected, and he continued to experience severe pain and discomfort. Despite the doctors' best efforts, the underlying damage caused by the acid leakage proved to be more extensive than initially thought.

Later, Nya got a call from Lola that her father was in the hospital, and he wasn't doing too good. Nya flew to Chicago to visit Henry in the hospital. As she sat in the airplane seat, her thoughts turbulent like the clouds outside the window. The plane taxied to the gate; her heart pounded with anxiety. She gathered her belongings and stepped into the terminal, her eyes scanning the crowd for any sign of her stepbrother Barry who was supposed to pick her up.

The drive to the hospital was a blur of honking horns and flashing lights, each passing moment filled with uncertainty. When they arrived, she walked to the elevator, her heart pounding in her chest, As the doors opened on the hospital floor, she saw the nurses rush past, doctors conferred in hushed tones, and families gathered in quiet desperation. She walked to Henry's room, where he lay motionless on the bed, hooked up to a tangle of tubes and wires. His face was pale and drawn, his breaths shallow and labored. She approached his bedside, her hands trembling as she reached out to touch his frail hand. His eyes fluttered open, and a weak smile tugged at the corners of his lips.

Tears welled in her eyes as she leaned in to embrace him, the weight of the situation crashing down around her. She reminisced about what he had done to her growing up, but she was here. She remained a constant presence at his side, drawing strength so she could forgive him. One day, after a series of tests, the devastating truth was revealed, it was too late. The acid had already wreaked havoc on Henry's internal organs, causing irreversible damage. The doctor delivered the news with a heavy heart, explaining that there was nothing more they could do to save him.

The family were all shattered by the grim prognosis. They struggled to come to terms with the reality that Henry was facing a battle that he could not win. Faced with the harsh realization that his time on this earth was limited.

Lola looked at Nya and said, "I know you have been through this before and it's hard going through it again," Nya said, "yes I have."

But the truth of the matter was, it was different from losing my mother. In fact, she really had no feelings at all even though he was her father. She was numb and she felt like something heavy had been lifted off her chest. Despite the overwhelming sorrow that engulfed them, Henry condition deteriorated further, family remained by his side, providing comfort and companionship until the very end. Though some hearts would ache with grief, they found comfort in the knowledge that Henry suffering would soon end, and hopefully he would find peace beyond this life.

In the quiet moments that followed, surrounded by loved ones, Henry found a sense of closure and acceptance. Nya wondered if he took comfort in his family surrounding him, knowing that he would forever be remembered for so many things he had done and how he had damaged some of their lives. The days passed, and Henry's journey ended. He passed away April 26, 2019.

Nya found herself enveloped in a complex mix of emotions. The loss of her father left a profound void in her life, one that seemed impossible to fill. Yet, amidst the grief and sorrow, there was an unexpected sensation that began to take root with her, a sense of relief. Nya found herself navigating a new reality, one where the weight of uncertainty and discomfort that had plagued her for so long began to dissipate. One without the constant worry about her father's abuse. A big release lifted off her shoulder; she no longer had to feel uncomfortable when she was around him and she no longer had to keep a secret anymore.

Chapter 27:
The Talk

As the sun dipped below the horizon, casting a golden glow over the city, the service for Henry had begun. The service had been a somber affair, filled with memories, tears, and laughter as friends and family shared stories of Henry. Lola felt a deep sense of sadness mingled with a strange peace as she watched out into the crowd. She stood beside the casket and made a speech about how Henry was such a good man and all he liked to do was work. She said that he was a hardworking man and all he wanted to do was to take care of his family, and that he would surely going to be missed.

Once the service concluded, guests began to disperse, offering condolences and warm embraces to Lola. Jocelyn, Nya's stepsister approached her with a serious expression etched upon her face.

"After this is over, we have to talk," Jocelyn said softly, her voice tinged with a hint of urgency.

Nya nodded, her brow furrowing with concern. "Of course, I'll be here. Just give me a call whenever you're ready."

With a hug and a brief squeeze of her hand, Jocelyn offered a small, sad smile before she turned and walked away, disappearing into the gathering crowd. As Nya watched Jocelyn leave, a whirlwind of emotions swirled in her head. Nya could not help but wonder what Jocelyn wanted to talk about, especially at a time like this. Was it something urgent? Did it involve Henry in some way? Unable to find answers to my questions, Nya took a deep breath and turned her attention back to the casket. In the stillness of the evening, she whispered a final goodbye to friends and family, her heart heavy with sorrow yet filled with gratitude.

When she turned around, Lola's sister Suzy was standing in front of her. She hugged her and asked how she was doing. They chitchatted for a bit and then she asked her,

"Had Henry ever touched you inappropriately before?" Nya was shocked because she was just approached by Jocelyn saying they needed to talk.

"Yes," Nya said.

"I thought so, because Jocelyn said the same thing happened to her." Suzy replied.

Now, she was really feeling sick to her stomach. After this service settled and everybody went back home. Nya had to call Joycelyn to find out what happened to her.

Nya called Jocelyn one evening to discuss what she wanted to tell her when they were at the funeral. When Jocelyn picked up the phone, Nya sensed the tension in her voice. It was not just grief; it was something else troubling her. As Jocelyn spoke, her words poured out like a dam breaking, revealing disturbing news. She told her how Henry would inappropriately touch her when she was sleeping sometimes, she would see something crawling on the floor next to where she would be lying in bed. She stated when she was washing dishes, how he would come behind her and rub up against her. Nya's mind flashed back because those were the same type of abuse she experienced.

Jocelyn recounted in an intense argument with Henry in the kitchen fueled by accusations and lies that she vehemently denied knowing anything about. But things took a terrifying turn when Henry, in a fit of rage, grabbed two-by-fours from the floor and struck her across the face with them. Shocked and scared, Jocelyn fled to a neighbor's house, refuge from the violence erupting in her house. Together, they went to the police station, where Jocelyn bravely recounted the harrowing ordeal to the officers. However, instead of receiving the support and protection she desperately needed, Jocelyn was subject to disbelief and dismissal.

The officer's callous comment, labeling Jocelyn as nothing more than a runaway child, cut deep. It was a cruel dismissal of her pain and trauma, reducing her to a statistic rather than recognizing her as a victim in need of help. Nya's heart ached for Jocelyn, imagining the fear and confusion she must have felt at that moment.

Jocelyn's heart pounded as she stood in the stark interrogation room, facing the officer who had just dismissed her trauma with a callous remark. Anger and fear surged within her as she confronted the indifference that permeated every corner of the room.

"What do you mean, 'runaway'?" Jocelyn's voice trembled with barely contained fury.

"I've just been assaulted by Henry, and you want to label me as a runaway? You would be running too if you were struck across the face with two-by-fours!"

The officer's smirk only fueled Jocelyn's indignation. His casual dismissal of her pain felt like salt rubbed into her wounds, and she refused to be silent by his indifference.

With a sense of defiance, Jocelyn squared her shoulders and met the officer's gaze head on. She refused to back down, refuse to let her suffering be brushed aside.

"Call her parent," the officer commanded, his

tone dripping with disdain.

Minutes later, Lola entered the room, her expression a mix of concern and apprehension. Henry remained outside, his absence a stark reminder of the rift that had torn the family apart.

The officer wasted no time, turning to Lola with a skeptical gaze. "Is she telling the truth?" he demanded.

Jocelyn held her breath, pinning her hopes on her mother Lola response. This was her chance for validation, for someone to finally acknowledge the pain she had endured.

"You better tell him the truth," Jocelyn's voice was a quiet but firm warning, her eyes locked with her mother's. "Or I will never speak to you again as long as I live."

Lola hesitated, caught between loyalty to Henry and the undeniable truth staring her in the face. But in the moment, faced with the unwavering resolve of her daughter, she knew what she had to do.

With heavy sigh, Lola admitted to the disagreement, her words a fragile bridge between truth and denial. She promised she would handle the situation, to make things right.

And true to her word, Lola took her home that

night, away from the toxic environment that had threatened to consume her. Lola made plans to send Jocelyn down south to stay with relatives until she finished high school, a temporary refuge from the storm raging within the family.

Nya told Jocelyn that she had no idea that she had moved down south or had any knowledge of what had happened to her. During this time, she did not visit as much. Nya told her that she was so sorry about having to go through that ordeal. She said the same to her. She also mentioned other relatives that she had heard that he'd done the same thing to them. Nya wondered who these other girls were because no one ever let on about being abused, like her. Everybody loved Henry. Nya stated he was an extremely sick man, and nobody did or said anything about it. Nya mentioned that Suzy asked her if he had abused her when she was growing up, and she said 'Yes."

"She mentioned that you told her that he had abused you too when they were at the funeral." Jocelyn was shocked because she said she never told anybody.

Nya wondered how Suzy knew. Now that she was older, she realized the only way to put a stop to girls being abused is to tell someone right away and get some help for their sanity. To not keep a secret because it only destroys you in the long run. Abusers make you feel like you have done something wrong when you have done nothing. She wished that as a child, she would have known this.

Chapter 28: The Last One

Now with so many of the family members gone, it was just Diana and Nya who carried the torch of memories and shared experiences. Every other week, like clockwork, they would call each other, those conversations becoming lifelines in an ever-changing world. Diana and Nya talked at least every other week. If she did not call, Diana would call her. Diana would always bring up the conversation about how things had changed. Life had taken many twists and turns since our childhood, but through it all, the connection with Diana remained a constant source of comfort and strength. Diana had always been like a big sister to Nya, the one who looked out for her and shared in her joys and sorrows.

One evening, Nya settled into her favorite place to sit, phone in hand, and dialed Diana's number. The familiar sound of the ringing brought a sense of anticipation, knowing that on the other end of the line was someone who understood her like no one else. Diana picked up after the second ring, her voice warm and welcoming.

"Hey there," she greeted, a smile evident in her tone. "How are you doing?"

"I'm good," Nya replied, a sense of relief washing over her. "How are you doing?"

"I'm doing alright," she said. "Just sitting here looking out the window and can't see shit."

Nya chuckled, imagining Diana sitting at the window being nosey.

The conversation flowed naturally, as it always did. They reminisced about the days when they were both young, even though she had some years on her, playing in the park and navigating the challenges of growing up in a big city.

Diana's voice softened as she shared memories of Grandma, her strength, and wisdom she imparted on both.

"Do you remember those summers when you and Mama used to spend down in Mississippi with Papa?" Diana asked, a hint of nostalgia in her voice.

"How could I forget?" Nya replied, smiling at the thought. "Those trips to visit Papa were some of the best times. His stories and the way the butterflies danced in the evening."

"Yeah, Diana agreed even though she didn't make those trips with Nya and Mama. "Those were simpler times. It feels like the world has changed so much since then."

A pause settled between Nya, both reflecting on how the world had indeed transformed. Trust seemed harder to come by, and the sense of community that once felt so strong had frayed in the fast-paced modern era.

"You know," Diana said, breaking the silence, "it's hard to trust anyone these days. People are different. Back then, you knew your neighbors, your community was like an extended family."

"You're right," Nya agreed. "It's like everyone is just trying to get by, and we've lost that connection. But I'm grateful we still have each other."

Diana's voice softened. "Me too. Especially now, with so many of our family gone. It's just you and I left to continue Mama's legacy."

Nya heart ached a little at the thought of those who were no longer with them, but there was also a profound sense of gratitude for Diana's presence in her life. She was her link to the past, the one who shared in her history and understood the depths of her loss.

"Tell me about how your bunch doing," Diana prompted, shifting the conversation to a lighter note.

They spent the next hour catching up on each other's lives, sharing stories of her children and grandchildren, their achievements, and the small triumphs and challenges of daily life. Diana talked about her grandchildren as well.

"I have some wonderful news," Nya said. "I'm coming to Chicago for my granddaughters High School Graduation, and I am coming to see you."

There was a brief pause at the other end, and then Diana's laughter filled her ears. "Well look at you! That's wonderful news. When are you coming?"

"In a couple of weeks," Nya replied. "I wanted to make sure I had enough time to visit you as well."

Diana sighed, a touch of weariness in her voice. "I'm not going to be doing nothing but sitting up in this house looking out the window."

Her words tugged at her heart. She knew how much Diana loved company, and how the days could sometimes feel long and lonely.

Determined to lift her spirits, she replied, "Well we're going to change that. When I get there, we're going to have some fun, just like old times."

Diana chuckled softly. "I like the sound of that."

As the evening grew darker outside my window, they both felt the comforting weight of the conversation. These calls were more than just updates, they were a way to keep the spirit of their family alive, to honor the memories of those who have passed, and to remind each other that they are never truly alone.

"Well," Diana said finally, "It's getting late. But I'm glad you called. I always feel better after our chats."

"Me too, Diana" I replied. "It's like a breath of fresh air. Take care, and we'll talk soon."

"Absolutely," she agreed. "Love you."

The week leading up to her trip to Chicago was supposed to be filled with joy and anticipation. Nya's granddaughter's graduation was a milestone event, and she was excited to celebrate her achievement and spend time with Diana. Nya had talked to Diana just a few days before, and she had expressed her excitement about her visit, even joking about how she was just sitting in her house looking out the window. But life has a way of throwing unexpected and heartbreaking twists into their plans.

It was a Wednesday evening, and Nya was busy packing her suitcase, carefully folding clothes and making sure she had everything she needed for the trip. The phone rang, breaking the quiet of her home. She picked it up, expecting to hear from a friend or a last-minute reminder from her granddaughter.

Instead, it was Diana's daughter Carolyn, her voice strained and filled with worry.

"Nya, it's me." She said, her tone was heavy with concern. "I have some sad news. My Mom had to be rushed to the hospital. She was complaining about severe stomach pains."

Nya heart sank once again, the sense of dread growing as she continued.

"The doctors found a bowel blockage and corrected it. She was doing okay for a while, but then things took a turn for the worse. She went into cardiac arrest. They managed to stabilize her, but one of her lungs collapsed, and she never came out of the coma. She passed away this afternoon."

Nya thought to herself, one by one, they're all gone. Diana was the last one to go. They kept each other laughing about things they used to do back in the day. First it was Raymond. He had been the spirited one, full of life and energy. But his life was tragically cut short when he was killed in a senseless act of violence. Then came Lance, whose struggle with AIDS was a battle that eventually claimed his life. Calvin's death was sudden and unexpected. His life was cut short by a seizure. Her mother Stella sudden stroke was a shock to everyone. Grandma Odessa, the matriarch of the family had lived a long and full life died in a nursing home. Hank had always been the one who looked out for everyone. But even he couldn't escape the march of time. Troy's death during the COVID-19 pandemic was a particular cruel twist of fate. And now, the last one, it was Diana's turn.

The world seemed to tilt; Nya's breath caught in her throat. "No, no," she whispered, tears streaming down her face. "Not Diana. She was supposed to be fine. I was coming to see her."

"I'm so sorry," Carolyn said, her own voice breaking. "I know how much you meant to each other."

A few days before Nya got on the plane, Carolyn called and said that she was making the funeral on a day that she was going to be in Chicago so that she would not have to stay long or make a second trip. So, the funeral was scheduled for 10:00 A.M on that Friday for the same day as the graduation ceremony. Luckily, the graduation was at 6:00 P.M that evening. Nya sat down, the weight of the news pressing down on her. The excitement of the upcoming trip turned into a sorrowful journey of loss. How could it be that she was now facing a day of such conflicting emotions? The joy of her granddaughters' achievement intertwined with the grief of losing Diana, the last of her grandmother's children. The whole clan was gone.

The days leading up to the trip were a blur of

preparations, phone calls, and tears. Nya tried to focus on the positive, the pride she felt for her granddaughter, but the shadow of Diana's loss loomed large. She kept replaying her last conversation with her in her mind, her laughter, her warmth, and her excitement about seeing her. When Nya arrived in Chicago, the city seemed different. The familiar streets and sounds that once brought comfort now felt muted under the weight of her grief. She was greeted by family members, all wearing expressions of shared sorrow and support.

The day of the funeral, a bittersweet blend of mourning and celebration. Nya dressed in the same outfit she had planned to wear for the graduation. The service was beautiful, a heartfelt tribute to Diana's life and the impact she had on everyone who knew her.

As she stood by her casket, tears streaming down her face, she whispered, "I told you I was coming to see you, but not like this. This was not the way I wanted to visit you."

Nya found comfort in the presence of family and friends who shared her grief, each person a testament to the love and connections that Diana had fostered throughout her life. Stories were shared, laughter mingling with tears as everyone remembered her kindness, her strength, and her unwavering support. Though Diana was no longer physically present, her spirit lives on in the stories, the memories, and the love that continued to bind her family. The pain of her loss was profound, but so too was the legacy she left behind, a legacy of love, resilience, and the unbreakable bond of family.

Nya's granddaughter's face lit up when she saw her, her joy was a bright spot in the midst of her sadness. As she walked across the stage to receive her diploma, Nya clapped and cheered, her heart swelling with pride. They took countless photos, wanting to capture every moment of her special day. For a few hours, she allowed herself to be swept up in the happiness of the occasion, surrounded by family and the achievement of the next generation.

As Nya prepared to leave Chicago, she took a moment to reflect on the intertwining of joy and sorrow that had marked her visit. Life had a way of weaving together the happiest and the hardest moments, and through it all, the love she shared with Diana remained a guiding light she knew that no matter where life took her, Diana memory would always be a part of her, a source of strength and inspiration.

Epilogue: Life's Lessons

Nya found comfort in the love of her grandma. She learned to cherish the moments they shared, to find joy in the simple pleasures of life, even as the unanswered questions continued to weigh heavily on her mind. It was not until years later, long after she had grown into a young woman with dreams of her own, that the pieces of the puzzle began to fall into place. Through a chance encounter and a series of unexpected twists of fate. She finally came face to face with her father, the man she had spent a lifetime wondering about. But not in the way she had hoped for.

In the hospital, she looked into his eyes and saw the echoes of guilt staring back at her. A flood of emotions washes over her anger, sadness, relief, and most of all overwhelming sense of forgiveness. She realized that the journey to understanding him was about finding answers and where to assign blame. It was about embracing the complexities of life, the messy tangle of what a father/daughter relationship should have been. When Henry passed, the weight of years began to lift from her shoulders, she knew that she was finally free, free to let go of the past, to embrace the present, and to forge a new future filled with hope, forgiveness, and love.

All these things affected her in some way or another. Though the journey was fraught with setbacks and challenges, she refuses to be defined by her past. With each step forward, she reclaimed a piece of herself that had been lost emerging from the shadows of abuse into the light of self-discovery and empowerment. She had weathered storms that would have broken most spirits. From the depths of loss to the pinnacle of triumph, her journey had been a symphony of trials and tribulations, each note playing a role in shaping the resilient soul she had become.

Once she was a fragile bud, easily swayed by the winds of adversity. But now, she stood tall, a testament to the strength that can be forged in the fires of hardship. It wasn't just the scars etched into her skin that told the story of her resilience; it was the way she carried herself with a quiet confidence born from countless battles fought and won.

People whispered tales of her, but never knew the other side of her, the girl who had stared down demons and emerged victorious. But to those who truly knew her, she was more than a myth, she was a beacon of hope in a world often covered in darkness.

She found herself on the other side of despair, basking in the warm glow of redemption. She had faced her demons, confronted her fears, and emerged stronger for it.

As she stood on the threshold of a new beginning, she knew that though the scars of her past would always remain, she was a survivor, a warrior, and nothing could dim the light that burned within her soul.

Ora Jackson is a retired Government Chief of Finance and author of "*Never Again*." She is married to Larry Jackson, a mother of three and seven grandchildren, who is proud that some followed her in Finance, the one who became an Author, and the ones still have time to decide which way they want to go. She is currently living in Las Vegas, Nevada.

Made in the USA
Columbia, SC
04 November 2024

a9fce30b-83f9-4fdc-9df0-7b1099f4babaR02